Number Sense and Nonsense

Number Sense and Nonsense

Building Math Creativity and Confidence Through Number Play

Claudia Zaslavsky

CHICAGO
REVIEW
PRESS

To all our children. I hope they will enjoy figuring out the difference between number sense and nonsense.

Library of Congress Cataloging-in-Publication Data

Zaslavsky, Claudia

Number sense and nonsense : building math creativity and confidence through number play / Claudia Zaslavsky.

p. cm.

Includes bibliographical references and index.

ISBN: 1-55652-378-5

1. Mathematics—Study and teaching (Elementary)—Juvenile literature. [1. Mathematical recreations.]   I. Title.

QA135.5 .Z368 2001

372.7—dc21   00-065872

Cover and interior illustrations and design: Rattray Design

©2001 by Claudia Zaslavsky
First Edition
Published by Chicago Review Press, Incorporated
814 North Franklin Street
Chicago, Illinois 60610
ISBN 978-1-55652-378-6
Printed in the United States of America
5 4 3 2

Contents

Acknowledgments

I want to thank the many educators and authors whose ideas I have adapted for this book. Several of their books are listed in the Bibliography. In particular, I am indebted to the *Family Math* book for the activity "Number Rectangles" on page 16. Beatrice Lumpkin informed me about the evidence for the concept of zero in ancient Egypt. The two-headed sheep on page 2 is described in *Finders, Keepers* by Stephen J. Gould and Rosamond Wolff Purcell (Norton, 1992). Credit for permission to reprint "The Monkey's Age," page 75, goes to Gary Hendren and the Missouri Council of Teachers of Mathematics *Bulletin* (March 1992).

Introduction

A Note to the Reader

This book is about numbers, all kinds of numbers. Numbers have different personalities, just like people. Numbers have relationships, just as people do. A person might be a daughter or son, a sister or brother, a cousin, and a friend. Numbers are also related to other numbers in various ways.

Some ways of connecting numbers make good *number sense*. Others may make no sense at all; they are just *nonsense*. In this book you will meet young people who are trying to tell the difference between number sense and nonsense. Often they

need some *common sense* to help them decide. I think you will enjoy their discussions and debates. You may want to have such discussions with your classmates, friends, and even grown-ups. These discussions will help you to build up your own number sense. You will develop a good head for numbers, the ability to see patterns in groups of numbers, and an appreciation of how useful numbers are and how much fun you can have with numbers.

Most of the topics in each chapter include ideas for activities that you can carry out either alone or with other people. There are also many questions for you to think about, questions that sometimes have no definite answers. Many of the activities are easy for you to check; you will decide whether they are correct. (See page 123–126 for the answers to some of the activities, although you probably won't need to refer to the answer pages very often. It's much more satisfying to work out the solutions yourself, even if it takes time.)

Some activities are harder than others, and may be too difficult for you to complete at present. Try them anyhow. Discuss them with your friends or a grown-up. Your *number sense* will grow as you work on them, even if you don't get the final answer correct. And you will feel so proud when you do work out a hard problem. But if you can't finish some of the activities now, come back to them next year, or the year after next.

You probably already know about odd and even numbers. But did you know that an odd number might be even, and an even number might be odd? Chapter 1 is all about odds and evens.

Chapter 2 introduces other relationships among numbers. You will have a chance to work on an idea, called a *conjecture*, about even numbers that no one has been able to prove either true or false,

although mathematicians have worked on it for over 200 years.

In Chapter 3 you will learn why zero is a very special number. For example, we cannot divide a nonzero number by zero. When I try to divide six by zero on my calculator, the display shows the word *error*. Zero is special in other ways, too.

Chapter 4 deals with money and decimal points and measures. You will learn how the United States lost hundreds of millions of dollars because of a mix-up in units of measurement.

Riddles and puzzles are the subject of Chapter 5, although you will also find some riddles and puzzles in other chapters. You will learn clever tricks with numbers that will make people think you are a genius!

How did numbers begin? How have people used numbers in the past? That's what Chapter 6 is all about. You will read about finger counting, number words in several languages, signs for numbers, and ways of calculating that have been used in different parts of the world over thousands of years.

You may wonder, what about the calculator? Why bother learning about numbers when the calculator can do all the work? Not true! The calculator has no *number sense*. It takes a human being to tell the calculator what to do. The same is true of the computer. But the calculator can be very useful, as you will find out in Chapter 7. You will learn about negative numbers, repeating and terminating decimal fractions, and a lot more.

Chapter 8 is about big numbers. Would you like your allowance to take the form of one cent on the first day of the month, two cents on the second day, four cents on the third day, eight cents on the fourth day, and double the amount every day until the end of the month? Guess how much money you would receive.

In the final section are lists of books for children and adults. Reading some of these books will help your number sense grow.

Happy reading, thinking, and talking about math!

A Note to Parents and Teachers

This book introduces groups of children having a wonderful time discussing, reflecting on, and arguing about mathematical ideas. These children discover that some ideas make good *number sense*, while other ideas do not make sense; they are just plain *nonsense*.

Math is for everyone! Research has shown that every child can learn math. When experienced through challenging activities, math can be a source of great joy and satisfaction to children and to adults. No longer can parents excuse their children by saying, "I was poor in math, so I am not surprised that Jennifer has trouble learning the subject." No longer can teachers justify their students' failure with the excuse: "Those kids can't learn."

We now know a great deal about how children learn. The British neuropsychologist Brian Butterworth believes that the brain has specialized circuits that he calls the "Number Module." In his fascinating and comprehensive book *What Counts: How Every Brain Is Hardwired for Math*, he writes, "There is nothing intrinsically dull or hateful about mathematics. It will be, and can be, fun, as long as children understand what they are doing and feel pride of ownership in mathematical ideas" (page 320; see the bibliography on page 127 of this book). He advises teachers to use "group discussions, encourage different solution strategies, acknowledge pupils' own intuitions and knowledge to stimulate inventiveness" (page 298). Of course, this advice is equally relevant for parents.

According to the *Principles and Standards for School Mathematics*, published in 2000 by the National Council of Teachers of Mathematics (NCTM), "Students learn more and better when they can take control of their learning. . . . When challenged with appropriately chosen tasks, students become confident in their ability to tackle difficult problems, eager to figure things out on their own, flexible in exploring mathematical ideas and trying alternative solution paths, and willing to persevere" (page 21). In other words, children must learn mathematics with understanding.

Unfortunately, much school instruction in mathematics has been based on rote memorization of facts and procedures, rather than on understanding. Memorized procedures are easily forgotten or confused, but the ability to reconstruct methods and arrive at solutions on the basis of mastering the underlying concepts remains with a person over the years.

As I write these words, educators and the public are caught in a dilemma. On one side are parents who feel that their children are being shortchanged because many of the current math programs do not call for extensive drill on multiplication tables and addition facts, the so-called "basics." On the other side are those who object to the kind of rote learning advanced by the older math programs, still used in many schools, and by teachers who teach as they have been taught, using "drill and kill" methods. With the increasing emphasis on standardized test scores, teachers are pressured to spend a great deal of time drilling for tests, in spite of the fact that research shows that when children learn the "basics" in the course of doing challenging math work, they are far better prepared to cope with new ideas than if they had learned by rote memorization methods.

This book focuses on numbers, their characteristics and relationships, applications of numbers in society, and the history of number systems. As recommended in the NCTM *Standards* (2000), readers also make connections to geometry and other branches of mathematics, they develop skills in estimation and problem solving, they generalize about patterns of numbers, and they are encouraged to engage in discussions with peers and adults (see pages 139–140). This book provides a model for creativity and independence in the learning of mathematics, and for the development of a positive attitude toward the subject.

The book is addressed to children in grades three to six, and encompasses a wide range of mathematical knowledge. I prefer not to specify a grade level or a level of difficulty for each activity. Children should be encouraged to try as many activities as possible. They should not be afraid to make mistakes or to follow a wrong path. Mathematicians do that all the time!

Odds and Evens

What This Chapter Is About

All whole numbers are divided into two groups—odd numbers and even numbers. They follow one another in order—odd, even, odd, even, like the page numbers in this book. But sometimes an even number can be odd, and an odd number can be even. You will read about it in this chapter.

Knowing how numbers behave can give a big boost to your *number sense*. That knowledge can help you discover when numbers are used in ways that make no sense, or are *nonsense*. You will learn when to expect an even number and when to expect an odd number as an answer to a problem in arithmetic.

The ancient Egyptians, almost 4,000 years ago, had a way of multiplying numbers using mostly even numbers. You will learn it, too.

When Is an Even Number Odd?

"A sheep with two heads!" exclaimed Eddie, pointing to a picture in the book he was reading. "That's an odd number of heads for an animal."

"That's *nonsense*," replied his sister Molly as she came over to look. "No animal has two heads! And what's more *nonsense*, two is not an odd number. Two is an even number."

"See, there really was such a sheep," said Eddie. "But you're right, an animal should have only one head. An animal with two heads is unusual. When I said 'an *odd* number of heads,' I meant that the sheep had an *unusual* number of heads."

Numbers like 1, 3, 5, 7, and 9 are called *odd* numbers. The numbers 2, 4, 6, and 8 are called *even* numbers. Are the odd numbers unusual? No, there are just as many odd numbers as even numbers. So why are these numbers called "odd"?

Words that describe numbers, like "odd" and "even," may also have other meanings. The dictionary gives many meanings for the word *odd*. One meaning is "left over after others are paired." Another meaning is "peculiar" or "strange."

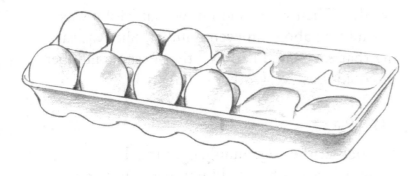

It makes *number sense* to call 7 an odd number. Think of seven eggs. Place them in a two-row egg carton so that you have three pairs. The one left over is the "odd" egg.

And it makes just plain common sense to call a sheep with two heads peculiar or strange or unusual.

How do you know whether a whole number is odd or even? We know that the one-digit numbers 1, 3, 5, 7, and 9 are odd, while 2, 4, 6, and 8 are even. How about larger numbers? Look at 825:

You know that 8 and 2 are even, while 5 is odd. But is 825 odd or even? How can you test the number?

- You can put 825 eggs in two-row egg cartons to find out whether one egg is left over after all the other eggs have been paired. But there is a better way.

- You can divide 825 by 2 and see whether there is a remainder. The answer is 412, with a remainder of 1. So 825 must be an odd number. But there is still a better way, a way that takes less time!

- Look at the digit in the ones place, the digit on the right. You know that 5 is an odd number. It means that 825 is an odd number. It makes good *number sense* to look at the digit in the ones place to decide whether a number is odd or even. It doesn't matter whether the other digits in the number are odd or even.

Try This

1. Is zero odd or even? How about numbers ending in zero, like 10 or 50?

2. Decide whether each number is odd or even. To test your answer, divide each number by 2. Is there a remainder?

426	807
250	999

When Is an Odd Number Even?

Molly and her five friends were about to share a box of cookies. There were 18 cookies in the box. She wondered whether every child would have the same number of cookies, with none left over.

Molly's class had not yet learned how to divide. She first gave each person one cookie, and then a second cookie. Some cookies were left in the box, and she gave each person a third cookie. Now the box was empty.

"It came out even," Molly said to her friends. "Everybody has three cookies and no cookies are left in the box."

When Molly said, "It came out even," did she mean that each child got an even number of cookies? That's *nonsense*. She knows that 3 is an odd number. Why did she say "even"?

The word *even* has many meanings, just as the word *odd* has many meanings. One meaning of *even* is "exact." Each child got exactly the same number of cookies, even though that number is odd. Molly might have said, "It came out evenly." Then we would know that Molly was not talking about an even number. She was saying that each child had exactly the same number of cookies as every other child.

Try This

1. Look at the page numbers in this book. Which pages have odd numbers? Which pages have even numbers? Find the pattern.

2. Do you or people you know live on a street on which every house has a number? Notice which numbers are even and which are odd. Find the pattern.

3. Write five telephone numbers, yours and those of your friends and relatives. Count the number of odd digits and the number of even digits. Are they about the same or is one group quite a bit larger than the other?

The Dating Problem

Some people write dates the short way, in numerals. Instead of March 27, 2001, they write 3-27-01, or 3/27/01. To save space, they write only the last two digits of the year: 01 instead of 2001.

When computers became popular, in the late 1900s, people saved space in the computer by writing a date like 1975 as just plain 75, using the last two digits. But that caused a big problem, called the Year 2000 problem, or Y2K problem. Many people were afraid that at the end of 1999, computers would record the next year as 1900 instead of 2000. That mistake might bring about terrible disasters, like shutting down water systems and electricity, and maybe setting off nuclear warfare! Billions of dollars were spent as the year 2000 approached to correct this error and avoid possible disaster.

Speaking of the year 2000 reminded Maria of a question she heard on the radio in the year 2000. She asked Eddie, "What is the earliest date starting in 2000 that has all even numbers when written in numerals?"

Eddie thought about it this way: "The year is 2000, and that's even. The first even-numbered month is February. So the date must be February 2, 2000, written 2-2-00."

"OK," said Maria. "Now tell me the last date before it that could be written with all even numbers."

"It can't be the year 1999, because that's an odd number. It must have been 1998. December is the twelfth month, and that's an even number. The date is December 30, 1998, written 12-30-98."

"Good thinking," replied Maria. "Try this one: What was the last date, before the year 2000, that could be written in numerals using only even digits?"

"Isn't it 12-30-98?" asked Eddie.

"Those are even *numbers*. I said all even *digits*."

Try This

Figure out the answer to the last question. Then ask this question of a friend or grown-up.

Number Sense About Odds and Evens

Knowing about odd and even numbers and how they behave can be a great help when you are working with whole numbers.

Kwan added the different kinds of cards in his collection:

$$12 + 26 + 8 + 16 = 63$$

Maria looked at his addition and in two seconds told him that he had made a mistake. His answer didn't make sense—it was *nonsense*. She didn't add the numbers. All she did was notice that all the numbers are even. Her *number sense* told her that the sum of even numbers is always even. Kwan's answer was an odd number, so it had to be wrong.

Number Sense in Addition

Here is a way that you can develop your *number sense*. Complete each sentence with the word *even* or *odd*. Try many examples before you decide.

- The sum of two even numbers is always _____.

- The sum of two odd numbers is always _____.

- The sum of one odd number and one even number is always _____.

Try This

Before you carry out each of the addition problems, decide whether the sum is odd or even. Then check your answer by doing the addition. You may want to use a calculator, but you will develop better *number sense* without the calculator. Even better, maybe you can do some of the addition in your head. That's called *mental arithmetic.*

8	35	64	77
32	25	106	60
15	24	320	149

Number Sense in Subtraction

Now let's see about subtracting, which is finding the difference between one number and another. Complete each sentence with the word *odd* or *even*. First try several examples of each type.

- The difference between two even numbers is always _____.
- The difference between two odd number is always _____.
- The difference between an even number and an odd number is always _____.

Does it matter whether the even number or the odd number is larger?

Try This

Ask a friend to write some subtraction problems. Then tell your friend, without doing the subtracting, whether the difference is odd or even using the subtraction rules you learned above.

Number Sense in Multiplication

When two numbers are multiplied together, the answer is called the product. Now complete these sentences with "odd" or "even":

- The product of two odd numbers is always _____.
- The product of two even numbers is always _____.
- The product of an odd number and an even number is always _____.

Knowing how odd and even numbers behave should help you to remember the multiplication facts.

Try This

1. Write the products for multiplying by 4: 4 × 1, 4 × 2, 4 × 3, and so on. That's the same as skip counting by fours. Then do the same for multiplication by 7: 7 × 1, 7 × 2, 7 × 3, and so on. Are the products odd or even? Do they follow a pattern?

2. Open a book and look at the page numbers of the two facing pages. Then open the book to another place and note the page numbers. Do this several times. Complete these sentences with the word *odd* or *even*:

- The sum of the two page numbers is always _____.
- The product of the two page numbers is always _____.

Number Sense in Division

This is a little more difficult to explain. When the answer comes out evenly, that is, when there is no remainder, you can figure out some rules. Use the multiplication facts to help you. You might want to work with a friend.

Using Number Sense and Just Plain Sense

Teacher: "Seven is an odd number. How can it be made even?"

Student: "Take away the S."

Puzzles About Odd and Even Numbers

Open-Book Puzzles

Here are some statements about the possible numbers on the two facing pages of an open book. The pages of the book are numbered in the usual way. Say whether each statement makes sense, or is *nonsense*.

1. The sum of the page numbers is 21.

2. The product of the page numbers is 380.

3. The product of the page numbers is 420.

4. The sum of the page numbers is 46.

5. The product of the page numbers is 99.

6. The sum of the page numbers is 99.

Make up some questions like these for your friend to answer. Try them out on a grown-up.

How Many Boys and How Many Girls?

Maria, Kwan, and Eddie were having a discussion about the number of boys and the number of girls in their class. Each one had a different opinion. Only one made *number sense*. The other two were talking *nonsense*. Decide which kid had a sensible answer, and why the other two didn't make any *number sense*.

1. Maria said there are 28 students in the class. There are five more boys than girls.

2. Kwan said there are 28 students in the class. There are four more boys than girls.

3. Eddie said there are 27 students in the class. There are four more boys than girls.

Multiplication by Doubling: The Ancient Egyptian Way

The ancient Egyptians must have liked to work with even numbers. They multiplied two numbers by doubling. We know that when any number is multiplied by two, the result is an even number. Then they kept right on doubling, as you will see in the example.

Suppose the problem is to multiply 14 by 13. This is how it was set up:

$$
\begin{array}{cc cc}
4 & 1 & \quad 4 & 14 \\
  & 2 & & 28 \\
4 & 4 & \quad 4 & 56 \\
4 & 8 & \quad 4 & 112 \\
\hline
\text{Sums } 13 & & & 182
\end{array}
$$

The product of 14 and 13 is 182.

★ Procedure

1. Set up two columns. Write the number 1 in the first column and 14 in the second column.

2. Multiply the numbers in both columns by two. Continue doubling until the next number in the first column would be greater than 13.

3. Check off the numbers in the left column that add up to 13.

4. Check off the numbers in the second column that are next to the checked numbers in the first column.

5. Add the checked numbers in the second column. This sum is 182, the product of 14 and 13.

Try This

1. For practice, multiply 13 by 14, using the Egyptian method of doubling. The first line of the two columns is:

$$
1 \qquad 13
$$

2. Find several more products by the Egyptian method. Make up your own numbers.

3. Figure out why the method works. Note that 13 = 1 + 4 + 8, so 14 × 13 = 14 × (1 + 4 + 8) = 14 + 56 + 112 = 182.

How do we know about ancient Egyptian multiplication? The Egyptians wrote on papyrus, and some of their original records remain.

Scientists learned to read the ancient Egyptian writing on papyrus, called hieratic writing.

An important source of this information is the papyrus of the scribe Ahmose (also called Ahmes), written more than 3,600 years ago. He began his papyrus with these words: "Accurate reckoning. The entrance into the knowledge of all existing things and all obscure secrets."

In a later chapter you will read how the ancient Egyptians and other people counted and wrote numbers long ago.

Prime and Not Prime

What's in This Chapter

Have you ever thought about a number as a rectangle of square tiles? Some numbers have several different rectangles. Some numbers have special rectangles called squares. By studying the rectangles you will learn about prime and composite numbers, about divisors and factors, about square numbers and multiples of numbers.

You will use a neat way to hunt for prime numbers, using a sieve to strain them out, while all the other numbers fall through the holes. You will test an idea about even numbers that people have been trying for over 250 years to prove either true or false. Maybe you will find the answer! You will learn to check your arithmetic by "casting out nines," and how to multiply by nine on your fingers.

Number Rectangles

Suppose you have a lot of small square tiles, each measuring one centimeter on the side. (If you don't use *centimeter* tiles, substitute the word *unit* for *centimeter*.) How many different rectangles can you make with three tiles? With four tiles? With a hundred tiles?

With three squares you can make just one rectangle.

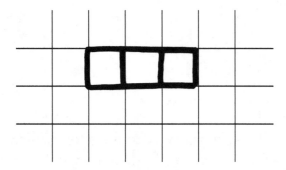

Its width is one centimeter and its length is three centimeters. No matter how you turn it, it remains the same rectangle.

You can form two different rectangles with four tiles.

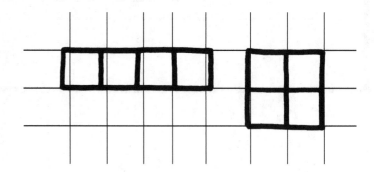

One rectangle is just one centimeter wide and four centimeters long. The other is a square; each side measures two centimeters. A *square* is a special kind of rectangle; all four sides are equal in length.

How many rectangles can you form with 100 squares? We'll tackle that problem a little later, but you might want to think about it in the meantime.

No matter how many tiles you start with, you can always make a rectangle that is one centimeter wide. The length is equal to the number of tiles you use. If you use three tiles, you can form a 1 × 3 (read it "one by three") rectangle. Of

Centimeter Grid

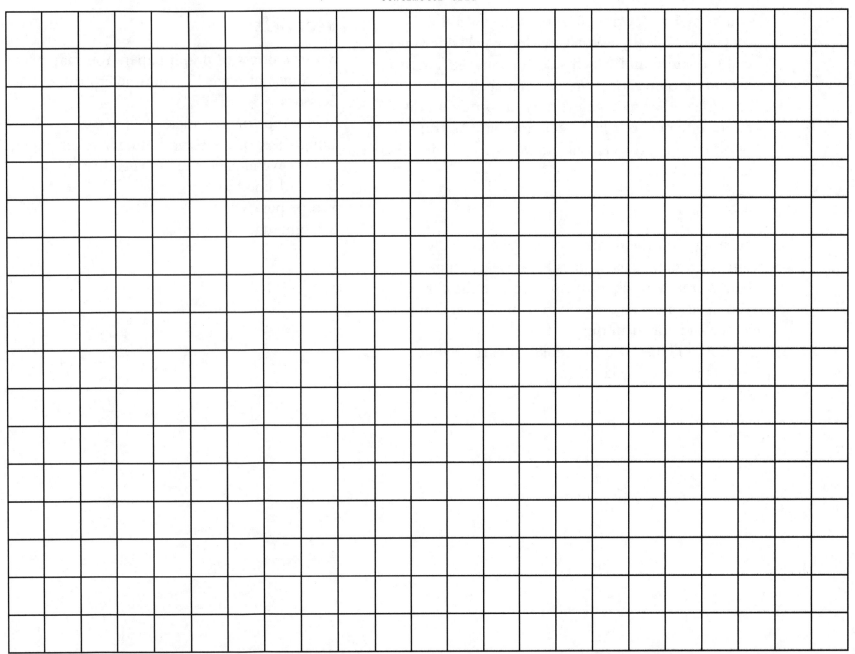

course, a 1 × 3 rectangle is the same as a 3 × 1 rectangle. It really doesn't matter which side you call the width and which side you call the length. You are looking for *different* rectangles.

What other rectangles can you form with different numbers of tiles? Let's find out. As you work on this project, your *number sense* will grow and grow!

Try This

Starting with the number one, make as many different rectangles as possible for each number. You may work with small square tiles, if you have them, or draw the rectangles on graph paper and cut them out.

You will also want to make a chart of your results to keep for later.

.Materials

Several sheets of graph paper. You may make copies of page 17 [centimeter grid]

Scissors

Sticky tape or gluestick

Long sheet of construction or butcher paper, or several sheets taped together

Sheet of lined paper

Pen or pencil

Straightedge or ruler

1. Form as many different rectangles as possible for as many numbers as possible beginning with the number one. Try to go up to at least the number 12.

2. Cut out each rectangle and tape or glue it to the construction paper. Your project should look something like this:

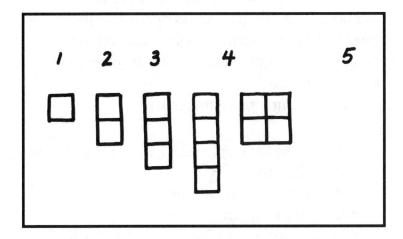

3. On lined paper, make a chart that looks like this:

Number	Rectangles	How Many Rectangles?
1	1 × 1	1
2	1 × 2	1
3	1 × 3	1
4	1 × 4, 2 × 2	2
5		

Figure 1

Keep this chart because you will need it later.

Think About This

1. Which numbers have only one rectangle, one centimeter wide?

2. Which numbers have rectangles that are two centimeters wide? What name do we give to these numbers?

3. Which numbers have more than two rectangles?

Prime and Composite Numbers

You can learn a great deal about numbers by looking carefully at the rectangles. To help you organize this information, make another chart. It should look like the chart in Figure 2.

Number	Divisors	Prime or Composite	Square
1	1	neither	yes
2	1, 2	prime	no
3	1, 3	prime	no
4	1, 2, 4	composite	yes
5			

Figure 2

You get the information from the chart in Figure 1.

There are special words to describe numbers and how they are related. They may be related in more than one way, just as a person might be a girl, a cousin to one person, a sister to another person, and a daughter to another.

You already know about odd and even numbers. The box on the next page has some more words to describe whole numbers. Treat this list as your little dictionary. You can refer to it whenever necessary.

Let's examine the number six.

- 6 has the divisors 1, 2, 3, 6. They are also called factors of 6.
- 6 is a composite number.
- 6 is not a square number.
- 6 is a multiple of 2 because 2 × 3 = 6.
- 6 is a multiple of 3 because 3 × 2 = 6.

The number *one* is considered neither prime nor composite.

Number Word Dictionary

- A *prime* number is a number larger than one that can be divided evenly (with no remainder) only by itself and one.
- A *divisor* of a number divides that number evenly (with no remainder). A divisor of a number is also called a *factor* of that number.
- A *composite* number has divisors besides itself and one.
- A *square* number has two divisors that are the same number. It is the product of two equal factors.
- A *multiple* of a number is the product of that number and another number larger than one.

Try This

Copy the chart in Figure 2.

1. Continue writing the numbers to at least 25.

2. Write all the divisors of each number. Use the chart in Figure 1 to help you find the divisors. Write them in order, from one to the largest.

3. Mark each number "prime" or "composite."

4. Write "yes" if the number is a square number, and "no" if it isn't square.

Think About This

Why is the number *one* neither prime nor composite?

All About Numbers

Lisa and Rasha worked together to make their number rectangles and charts like those in Figure 1 and Figure 2. They were surprised to learn how much there was to know about numbers.

Try This

Rasha and Lisa looked at the numbers from 1 to 25 in the chart. Here are some of the things they found. You can find them, too.

1. Name the square numbers.

2. Make a list of the prime numbers.

3. Name the numbers that have exactly three divisors.

4. Name the numbers that have exactly six divisors.

5. What can you say about a number that has an odd number of divisors?

6. List the numbers that have 3 as a *common* factor. List the numbers that have 5 as a *common* factor.

7. Name the smallest number that is a *common* multiple of both 3 and 5.

8. List all nine divisors of 100. How many different rectangles can you form with 100 square tiles?

Think About This

Describe the connection between the number of rectangles and the number of divisors of any number. When you think you know the connection, check it out by testing it with many different numbers in the two charts, Figure 1 and Figure 2.

What's Odd About Adding Odd Numbers?

Rasha was making patterns with her small square tiles. First she put down one red tile, one little square. Then she made a bigger square. She laid a yellow tile next to the first square, another yellow at the corner, and a third yellow next to it, to make a 2 × 2 square. Then she made a still bigger square. She laid two blue tiles along one edge of the 2 × 2 square, two blues along the next edge, and one blue in the corner between them, to make a 3 × 3 square, as in Figure 3.

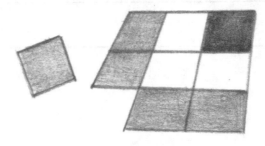

R = red
Y = yellow
B = blue

Figure 3

Rasha began to notice a very interesting pattern. She decided to make a chart to show the pattern.

Number of Tiles

Square	Add
O	1
$1 \times 1 = 1$	3
$2 \times 2 = 4$	5
$3 \times 3 = 9$	

Try This

Follow Rasha's example to make bigger and bigger squares. If you don't have square tiles, draw the small squares on graph paper. How large a square can you make? Then make a chart to show what you did.

.Materials

Small square tiles of several colors, or a
   sheet of centimeter grid paper (page 17)
Sheet of lined paper
Pencil or marker
Ruler

Think About This

What pattern about odd numbers did you discover as you made your chart?

Hunt for Primes

You can learn a really neat and easy way to hunt for prime numbers. It is called the sieve of Eratosthenes. Eratosthenes was born more than 2,000 years ago in Cyrene, a city in North Africa. He spoke and wrote in the Greek language, as did many scientists at that time.

A *sieve* lets liquid flow through and strains out solid pieces, just as you might strain bits of pulp from orange juice. Eratosthenes invented a sieve to strain out prime numbers. This is how it works for the numbers from 1 to 25. Set up your own diagram, as in Figure 4:

1	2	3	4	5	6	7	8	9	10
11	12	13	14	15	16	17	18	19	20
21	22	23	24	25					

Figure 4

★ *Procedure*

1. Draw a circle around 2, the first prime number. Then cross out every second number, starting with 2. These are the multiples of 2, the even numbers. You are skip counting by twos.

2. Draw a circle around 3, the next prime number. Cross out every third number, starting with 3. These are the multiples of 3. You are skip counting by threes. You have already crossed out the multiples of 3 that are also multiples of 2, such as 6 and 12.

3. You have already crossed out 4.

4. Draw a circle around 5, and cross out every fifth number. You will find that you have already crossed out all the multiples of 5 except 25.

5. Continue until you have drawn circles around all the prime numbers less than 25. You should find nine primes. Was it easy to pick out the primes bigger than 5?

Try This

Photocopy the 100 chart on page 27, or draw your own 100 chart. Follow the procedure to find all the prime numbers less than 100. You should find 25 prime numbers.

Think About This

Notice that you can stop counting multiples after you have crossed out the multiples of 7. Why don't you need to cross out multiples of 11? Think about this, and try to explain the reason to a friend or your parent.

100 Chart

1	2	3	4	5	6	7	8	9	10
11	12	13	14	15	16	17	18	19	20
21	22	23	24	25	26	27	28	29	30
31	32	33	34	35	36	37	38	39	40
41	42	43	44	45	46	47	48	49	50
51	52	53	54	55	56	57	58	59	60
61	62	63	64	65	66	67	68	69	70
71	72	73	74	75	76	77	78	79	80
81	82	83	84	85	86	87	88	89	90
91	92	93	94	95	96	97	98	99	100

Those Even Numbers

"Do you know what I learned about numbers?" Lisa asked her friend Rasha as they sat eating cookies one day after school. "My brother said that every even number greater than two is the sum of two prime numbers."

"Wow! That sounds impossible! Maybe he's just kidding you and it's really *nonsense*," replied Rasha.

"Well, I found that it worked for the first few even numbers." Lisa wanted to test the idea with more even numbers. Rasha was ready to go along. She started with the number four.

"Let's see. The first even number bigger than two is four. Four is two plus two, and two is a prime number. Can you use the same number twice?"

"Oh, sure."

"The next even number is six. How about two plus four?"

"That's not right. Four is not prime. Besides, don't you see that it makes no sense to add two to a different prime number to get an even number? That's really *nonsense*!"

"I don't understand," complained Rasha. "Why is it nonsense?"

"Think about this. Two is an even number. All the other prime numbers are odd. The sum of an even number and an odd number is always odd, isn't it? We want sums that are even numbers."

Rasha thought for a minute. "Hey, you're right. So we can forget about using two. Now let's get back to six. Three plus three equals six."

"And eight is three plus five."

"And ten is three plus seven," Rasha called out, while at the same time Lisa said, "Ten is five plus five." The girls looked at each other and laughed. They had found two different answers, both correct.

Rasha was becoming really excited. "Let's make a list of the prime numbers. Then we will know which numbers we can use."

Rasha wrote the list of primes: 2, 3, 5, 7, 11, 13, 17, 19. . . . Meanwhile, Lisa started a list of even numbers. As they worked out the sum for each even number, she wrote it down:

$$4 = 2 + 2$$
$$6 = 3 + 3$$
$$8 = 3 + 5$$
$$10 = 3 + 7 = 5 + 5$$

After the girls had written sums of all the even numbers up to 50, Rasha said, "How do we know whether it's true for all the even numbers? There is an infinite number of even numbers. We can't test them all."

Lisa thought for a while. "That's true, no one can test *all* the even numbers, not even with a computer. My brother said that if someone found an even number where it doesn't work, that would be proof that the idea is false. That hasn't happened."

This idea is called Goldbach's conjecture. A *conjecture* is an idea that has not been proved either true or false. Goldbach, a Prussian (German) mathematician, proposed this idea back in the year 1742. People have been trying to prove or disprove it ever since.

Try This

Continue the list that Lisa and Rasha started.

1. Make a list of the prime numbers, as far as you want to go.

2. Make a list of the even numbers, as far as you want to go.

3. Write the sum of two prime numbers that equals each even number. Try to find more than one way to do this, if possible.

Think About This

Goldbach had another conjecture. He thought that every odd number greater than five can be expressed as the sum of three prime numbers. The same prime can be used more than once in a sum. How far can you go to test this idea? For example, $9 = 2 + 2 + 5 = 3 + 3 + 3$.

Factors of a Number

Lisa and Rasha were having their cookies and milk after school one day.

Lisa remarked, "Do you remember that book, *The Doorbell Rang*, about sharing cookies? Every time they figured out how many cookies each kid would get, the doorbell rang and more kids came in to share the cookies. Suppose they made a really big batch of cookies. Is there an easy way to know whether each person will have the same number of cookies without having to do all the division?"

"You are asking whether there is an easy way to know whether a certain number is a factor of another number. Like if the number is even, you know that two is a factor of that number, and the number is divisible by two."

"Yeah, that's the idea," replied Lisa. "Let's write down what we know already about numbers and their factors."

Another way to state their question is to ask how to test that a number is divisible by another number. It means that when you divide the larger number by the smaller, there is no remainder. They made a list:

- 2 is a factor if the ones digit is an even number.
- 5 is a factor if the ones digit is 0 or 5.
- 10 is a factor if the ones digit is 0.

The girls noticed that 2 and 5 are factors of 10, the most important number in our system of numbers. In fact, we say that 10 is the *base* of our number system.

Rasha and Lisa wondered about other one-digit numbers, and decided to do some research. This is what they learned:

- 3 is a factor if the *sum of the digits* is a multiple of 3.
- 4 is a factor if the *last two digits* on the right are a multiple of 4.
- 6 is a factor if 2 and 3 are both factors.
- 9 is a factor if the *sum of the digits* is a multiple of 9.

They also learned that the test for 7 and 8 takes more work. It's often easier just to do the division.

The girls decide to test a big number, 4,680:

- 4,680 is divisible by 2 because the units digit is an even number.
- 4,680 is divisible by 3 because 18, the sum of 4 + 6 + 8 + 0, is a multiple of 3.
- 4,680 is divisible by 9 because the sum of the digits is a multiple of 9.
- 4,680 is divisible by 6 because it is even and is divisible by 3.
- 4,680 is divisible by 4 because 80 is divisible by 4.
- 4,680 is divisible by 5 and by 10 because the last digit is 0.
- 4,680 is divisible by 18 because it is even and divisible by 9.

Try This

Choose a large number and test it for divisibility by one-digit numbers. Then check it out by carrying out the division.

Casting Out Nines

While Rasha and Lisa were looking for information about divisibility tests, they came upon the trick called "Casting Out Nines." This is a way of checking your work in addition, subtraction, and multiplication. The Arabs were using it more than a thousand years ago.

The girls tried it out with each operation. Here are the examples they used. For each number, they found the sum of the digits. If the sum of digits is greater than 9, add the digits in this sum, until the final sum is a one-digit number, called the *digital* of the number.

Addition:	*Numbers*		*Digitals*
892 ⟶ 19 ⟶ 10 ⟶			1
25 ⟶			7
+179 ⟶ 17 ⟶			+8
1,096 ⟶ 16 ⟶ 7		16 ⟶	7

The digital of the sum is 7 in both columns. It seems that the addition is correct.

To check subtraction, subtract the digitals. To check multiplication, multiply the digitals.

(Caution: Sometimes this method doesn't work.) Lisa added like this:

$$258 + 479 = 647$$

The "casting out nines" test worked, so the answer seemed correct. Both sums had the digital 8. But when Rasha looked at the addition, she saw that it was incorrect.

"The correct sum is 737," she told Lisa. The girls wondered what went wrong.

Try This

Use "casting out nines" to test several calculations. Try it with addition, with subtraction, and with multiplication.

Think About This

Figure out why the test did not work for Lisa's addition.

Your Fingers as a Calculator

Rasha showed her father the "casting out nines" trick. That reminded him of a trick he learned when he was a boy. He said, "I'll show you how to multiply by nine using your fingers. No paper or pencil, no calculator."

"Let's see you multiply 9 times 364 on your fingers, " challenged Rasha.

"I can't do that. It only works for multiplication with any number 2 to 10. Here's what you do."

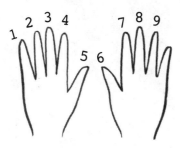

He held up his fingers. "Number your fingers from 1 to 10. Suppose you want to multiply 9 times 4. Bend the fourth finger. Now count the fingers to the left of the bent finger—

3. There are 6 fingers to the right of the bent finger. The answer is 36. Now you try it."

Rasha used her fingers to multiply 9 × 8.

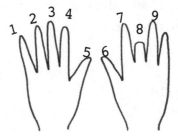

She counted 7 fingers to the left of the bent finger and 2 to the right. The answer: 72.

Try This

Use your fingers as a calculator to multiply nine times any number from 2 through 10. Figure out why it works.

Think About This

1. When you skip count by nines—9, 18, 27, 36, . . . notice the patterns in the tens digit and the units digit as the numbers grow larger. Also notice the digital, the sum of the digits of the number. Use these ideas to help explain why finger multiplication works.

2. Here is another way to multiply any number by 9; for example, 9 × 28:

    (1) Multiply the number by 10: 10 × 28 = 280 (do it mentally).

    (2) Subtract the number from the product: 280 – 28 = 252. Why does it work?

Zero—Is It Something? Is It Nothing?

3

What's in This Chapter

Words and signs for zero were invented long after people had made up words and symbols for numbers like one, two, and three. Zero is a special number in many ways, as you will learn in this chapter. Sometimes zero means something, other times it means nothing. Sometimes zero changes another number, other times it doesn't, as you will see when you make your own odometer. Our place-value number system would not work without zero. But don't try to divide by zero—it can't be done.

That Funny Number

"I have a poem about a number," Abdul said to his younger brother David. "See whether you can figure out what number the poem is about."

*I know a funny number. Can you guess
    its name?
When added to another, that other
    stays the same.
Subtract it from another; the other
    doesn't change.
There's more about my number that
    makes it seem so strange.
When multiplied by a million, my
    number doesn't budge.
I just can't think of anything to
    give my number a nudge.
Divide it by two, by five, by six;
    the answer is, again,
The number that I started with.
    Can you name it, then?*

"That can't be a number!" exclaimed David. "Numbers always do something when you add them or multiply them, or whatever. You're talking *nonsense*."

"There really is such a number," his brother replied. "It's called zero. I'll show you how it works."

Abdul read each part of the poem out loud to show David that it really made good *number sense*.

When added to another, that other stays the same.

"I have two coins in my right hand. I have no coins—zero coins—in my left hand. Altogether, in both hands, I have two coins. Two plus zero equals two."

$$2 + 0 = 2$$

Subtract it from another, the other doesn't change.

"Oh, I get it!" said David. "I counted 70 cents in my penny bank yesterday. I haven't taken out any pennies since then. I took out zero pennies. Seventy minus zero equals 70. I still have 70 cents in the bank."

$$70 - 0 = 70$$

When multiplied by a million, my number doesn't budge.

David wondered about that. "When you multiply by a million, you should get a really big number as an answer. How can the answer be zero?"

"Imagine a million glasses, all empty. No liquid in the first glass, no liquid in the second glass, no liquid in the millionth glass—zero amount of liquid in each glass. A million times zero equals zero. Any number times zero equals zero."

$$1,000,000 \times 0 = 0$$

Divide it by two, by five, by six; the answer is, again, the number that I started with.

"I think I can explain that," said David. "I believe there is a pint of ice cream in the fridge. We can divide it between the two of us. But if the ice cream is gone, then there are zero pints of ice cream in the fridge—divide zero by two. You get no ice cream and I get no ice cream. We each have zero amount of ice cream."

$$0 \div 2 = 0$$

"Good thinking," answered Abdul. "Let's see if there really is ice cream in the fridge."

Try This

Make up one or more stories for using zero in each operation: addition, subtraction, multiplication, and division. They can be short stories, like this one told by Kathy and David. Ask a friend whether your stories make *number sense*, or are they *nonsense*.

Ghosts

The next day, David went to school feeling very smart. On the way he met his friend Kathy. She was all excited.

"Do you know what, David?" Kathy asked. "There were ghosts in our house last night!"

"Ghosts, Kathy?" David asked. "I bet our house has 10 times as many ghosts as yours!"

Who is telling the truth? Who is not telling the truth?

Kathy is not telling the truth. She is teasing David. She knows that there are no ghosts. Kathy's house has zero ghosts.

David is telling the truth. Ten times zero is zero. David's house has zero ghosts, too.

How many ghosts have you seen in your house?

When Is Zero Something?

As Abdul and David were walking home from school, David looked at the house numbers on their street: 402, 404, 406, 408, and 410. He noticed that every number had a zero in it. He wondered what would happen if he took away the zero from each number: 42, 44, 46, 48, and 41. "That wouldn't make sense. That's *nonsense!*" he said aloud.

"What's nonsense?" asked Abdul.

David explained what he had discovered. "I looked at the number on the house on the corner—402. You said that if you take away zero from a number, that number stays the same. But 42 is not the same as 402."

Abdul thought for a while. Then he explained to David, "You are thinking about subtraction. Sometimes it means that you take away a number from another number. If you subtract zero from 402, the answer is 402. But if you remove or cross out the zero in 402, the number is changed to 42, a different number."

"Well, that makes *number sense*. Now I see that zero can be something."

"Next time you ride in the front of the car, look at the odometer. The odometer is a counter. It tells you how many miles the car has traveled."

David did look at the odometer the next time he was in the car. The odometer had room for six digits. He read:

004068

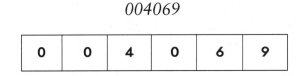

He watched as the odometer reading changed to

004069

| 0 | 0 | 4 | 0 | 6 | 9 |

Then the reading changed to

004070

| 0 | 0 | 4 | 0 | 7 | 0 |

He knew that the car had traveled 4,070 miles.

Which zeros mean something?

Which zeros mean nothing?

First David mentally crossed out the first two zeros. The number of miles was 4,070. The number hadn't changed.

Then he removed the next zero. The number was now 470. The number had changed. That zero means something.

Then he removed the last zero. The number was now 47. The number had changed again. That zero also means something.

0̸ 0̸ 4 0 7 0

0̸ 0̸ 4 0̸ 7 0

0̸ 0̸ 4 0̸ 7 0̸

Try This

Find examples of numbers that have zeros that mean something. Find numbers that have zeros that mean nothing.

Make Your Own Odometer

You can make a counter, called an odometer.
Ask a grown-up to help you.

.Materials

Sheet of heavy paper
4 strips of heavy paper, each 1 inch (2.5 cm)
   wide and 11 inches (28 cm) long
Sticky tape or gluestick
Scissors
Marker or pen
Ruler

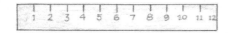

On each strip of paper:

1. Mark off 11 equal spaces by drawing 10
   lines, one inch (2.5 cm) apart.

2. Write the numbers 0 through 9.

3. Leave the last space empty.

On the sheet of paper:

4. Rule four 2-inch (5-cm) -wide columns.

5. Into each column, cut two slits, 1 inch (2.5
   cm) wide and 1 inch (2.5 cm) apart.

Thousand 1000	Hundred 100	Ten 10	One 1
—	—	—	☐
—	—	—	

Figure 1

0
1
2
3
4
5
6
7
8
9

Push one strip of paper through each pair of slits in each column.

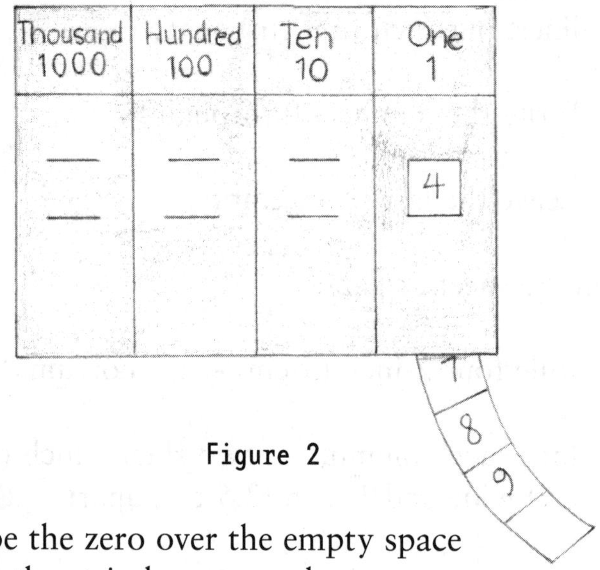

Thousand 1000	Hundred 100	Ten 10	One 1
— —	— —	— —	4

Figure 2

Tape the zero over the empty space so that the strip becomes a loop.

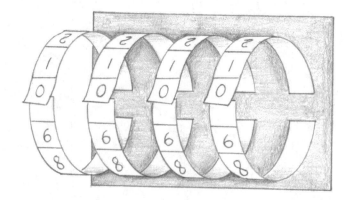

Figure 3

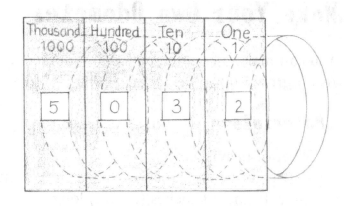

Figure 4

Now you can show any number from 0 to 9,999.

The Many Uses of Zero

Not only is zero a number, it's a very useful number. Here are some of the ways that zero is used.

Zero Means Nothing

No money, no homework, no television—just zero of all these things.

Zero as a Placeholder

You need to use a zero when you write numbers in our place-value system. How do you write the number "four hundred six"? You write 406. The zero shows that there is nothing in the tens place.

Zero in Round Numbers

How many children attend your school? If you are not sure of the exact number, you might say "about 400" or "about 800." What is the diameter of the Earth at the equator? It's hard to remember the correct number—7,926 miles—so we *round it off* to 8,000 miles. Round numbers usually end in zeros. They tell *about* how many or *about* how much.

Zero as the Starting Point of a Scale

Look at a ruler. The scale starts at zero. Sometimes the zero is not marked on the ruler. You must start measuring at zero to get the correct length.

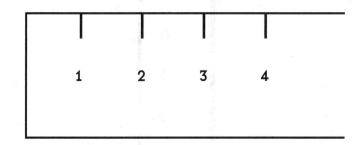

Zero to Separate Positive and Negative Numbers

Fifty degrees below zero! Brrr, that's really cold. Think of the scale on a thermometer as a number line. The temperatures above zero are positive and the temperatures below zero are negative. Zero separates the two kinds of numbers, the positive numbers from the negative numbers. Check it out on a real thermometer.

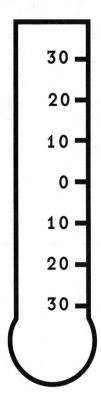

Zero in the Countdown

10, 9, 8, 7, 6, 5, 4, 3, 2, 1. BLAST OFF on zero! Soon the spaceship is in orbit around the Earth.

Zero Before a Decimal Point

You may have seen a number written as 0.3. You read 0.3 as "three-tenths." The zero reminds you to watch for the decimal point. It is also correct to write three-tenths as .3, but it is easier to make a mistake this way because you may miss the decimal point.

Is 0 a Number or a Letter?

As Kathy said good-bye to her friend Aviva, she added, "Call me later about the party. Write down my number: Two eight seven, three two four oh."

After supper, Aviva pressed the buttons on her telephone. A man answered, "Hello. This is the Super TV Service. What can I do for you?"

"I want to talk to Kathy," said Aviva.

"Sorry. There is no Kathy here. You must have the wrong number."

Aviva tried again. The same man answered the phone. "What number do you want, young lady?" Aviva read the number to him, just as Kathy had given it to her.

"I'm sorry," said the man. "Our number is two eight seven, three two four *six*. You pressed six instead of zero."

Look at the telephone keypad to see why Aviva pressed 6 instead of 0. She thought that Kathy meant the *letter* "O." Kathy really meant the *number* "0." People often say "oh" when they mean "zero" in a phone number.

Try This

1. Look at the telephone keypad. Find the letter O. Then find the number 0. Do they both have the same shape, or different shapes? Read the word printed below the numeral 0.

2. Look at license plates when you are out walking. Can you always tell whether the license number has the letter O or the number 0?

The Missing Year

How old were you at the moment you were born? Your age was zero years, zero months, zero days, zero hours, and zero minutes. You were not one year old until a year after your birth. But the calendar we use has a different story.

About 1,500 years ago the Christian calendar was invented in Europe. At that time, people didn't think much about zero. In fact, they had no symbol for zero. They started the calendar with the year one as the year in which Christ was born. They wrote the letters A.D. with the number of the year. A.D. stands for the Latin words *Anno Domini*, meaning "in the year of the Lord." For example, they would write A.D. 527. Two centuries later, people began to think about the years before the birth of Christ. They talked about the years 1 B.C. (Before Christ), 2 B.C., and so on. The time line looks like this:

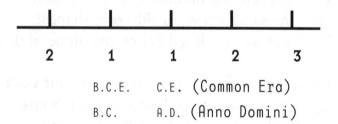

Today some people write C.E. (in the Common Era), instead of A.D., for the years

starting with the year 1. For the years before year 1, they use B.C.E. (Before the Common Era). People in other parts of the world use other calendars: Jewish, Chinese, Muslim, and many others. All these calendars start in different years.

Try This

1. In our calendar, how many years passed between the year 2 B.C.E. and the year 2 C.E.?

2. Draw a time line for a calendar that has a year zero, and years before and after year zero. How many years passed between the year 2 B.C.E. and the year 2 C.E. in this calendar?

3. Find information about a calendar that starts in a different year from that of the Christian calendar. You might look at the Chinese, the Muslim, or the Jewish calendar.

Think About This

During the year 1999, there was much discussion about the new century and the new millennium (1,000 years). Did it start with the year 2000 or the year 2001? What do you think? Ask other people what they think. Does one year make better *number sense* than the other as the starting point? Of course, 2,000 is a nice round number, with all those zeros, and people like round numbers.

Who Wrote the First Zero?

The ancient Egyptians invented number symbols more than 5,000 years ago (see page 85). They didn't need a zero to write these numerals because they didn't need a placeholder. For example, they wrote "three hundred two" as:

11999

They wrote three signs for "one hundred" and two signs for "one."

But the Egyptians did use the idea of zero in other ways. One way was in keeping track of things. Suppose that five bags of grain were brought into the king's storage house at the beginning of the day, and all five bags of grain are used up. How much grain is left in the storage house? No bags of grain. The keeper of the records wrote the symbol:

Another use of zero was in measurement. Scientists have found horizontal guidelines that the Egyptians used to help in the construction of pyramids. The line at the level of the ground showed the symbol meaning zero. Each of the other lines had a number symbol showing the number of units above zero or below zero. These lines must have helped the builders in their measurements of the pyramid and its foundation.

Over 2,000 years ago, symbols for zero appeared as placeholders in numerals in two different parts of the world. The surprising thing is that the two peoples who invented these symbols lived thousands of miles apart. Both these peoples had systems of written numbers that used place value.

The Maya, in Mexico and Central America, had a zero symbol that looked like a shell (see page 48). It might appear inside the numeral or in the last place, the ones place. In Mesopotamia (also called Sumer, now Iraq), two small slanting lines were used inside a numeral, but not at the end of a numeral.

Centuries later, a symbol for zero, like a small *o*, appeared in India as part of their number system. Arabic traders and travelers brought the symbol to other parts of Asia and Africa. More centuries later, Indo-Arabic numerals, along with the zero symbol, became popular in Europe. Today, most of the world uses this system.

Zero has been written in different ways.

The ancient Egyptians wrote

The Maya wrote

The Mesopotamians wrote

The people of India wrote

Now we write

The calculator shows

Some computers print

Zero Is a Special Number

It is not surprising that many centuries passed before people considered zero to be a number like the numbers that had been used for ages. Zero really is a special number.

Is zero an even number or an odd number? To find out, divide zero by two. The answer is zero, and there is no remainder. So zero must be an *even* number.

You know that you can divide zero by two or six or some other number, and the answer will always be zero: $0 \div 6 = 0$.

Can you divide a nonzero number by zero? Use your calculator to try to divide six by zero. The answer space will probably show the word *error*, or an *E*, which means "error." Let's figure out why this is so. Pay close attention to this example.

You know that multiplication and division are connected. For example:

$$3 \times 2 = 6, \text{ so } 6 \div 3 = 2$$

Now let's start with division by zero, and use multiplication to find the answer. Let's divide six by zero. We'll call the answer *N*, and use multiplication to figure out what *N* is.

$$6 \div 0 = N, \text{ so } 0 \times N = 6$$

What number is *N*? We know that zero times a number is zero, not six. There is no number that makes zero times that number equal six.

But can you divide zero by zero? If you have a calculator, punch in "zero divided by zero." In the answer space you will probably see the word *error*, or an *E*. Actually, $0 \div 0 = 2$ or 5 or ½ or 1,000,000 or any number! Use multiplication to check it out.

So we don't divide by zero. Division by zero doesn't make sense. Division by zero is *nonsense*.

What Is a Googol?

How many zeros are in this number?

10,000,000,000,000,000,000,000,000,
000,000,000,000,000,000,000,000,
000,000,000,000,000,000,000,000,
000,000,000,000,000,000,000,000

Try to find an easy way to count the zeros, without having to count every single zero.

The number is called a *googol*. A nine-year-old boy made up the name for this number. Now everyone calls this number a googol.

Money, Measures, and Other Matters

What's in This Chapter

In this chapter you will use your *number sense* to solve some problems about money. How can you get the best deal when you shop? You will discover how handy it is to know how to estimate an answer to a problem. You will find out about Tom Fuller, a slave called the "African Calculator" because of his ability with numbers. You will learn how the ancient Egyptians figured out equal shares. Why is a decimal point necessary? Whose feet are used for measuring? And why do you need *common sense*, as well as *number sense*, when you solve problems?

Lastly, you will find out about a mix-up in units of measurement that cost United States taxpayers millions of dollars.

Choose the Better Deal

Trisha and Samantha were shopping for bubble gum. The price of Big Bubble gum was two for a nickel, while three pieces of Fruitie gum cost a dime. Which gum should the girls choose, to spend the least money and get the most gum?

"Look, Sam," said Trisha, "Big Bubble is a better deal. You get two for a nickel. That means you can buy four pieces for two nickels, or four **for a dime**. That's cheaper than three for a dime."

Meanwhile Sam was doing some figuring in her head. "If you get two for a nickel, you pay two and half cents for each piece. Three for a dime means each piece costs three and a third cents. You're right, Big Bubble is cheaper. Let's buy some Big Bubble gum."

Trisha wasn't that good with fractions, but she knew that a price of a bit more than three cents was more than a price of two and half cents. Then she had another idea. "Look, Sam, the Fruitie pieces are bigger than the Big Bubble pieces. Maybe Fruitie is a better deal."

"That's true, Fruitie pieces are bigger. But how much gum do you need to make bubbles? Big Bubble is big enough."

That settled it. The girls each bought five cents worth of Big Bubble.

Then Samantha saw that Sweetie-Sweet candy was on sale for 15 cents a package, reduced from 25 cents. She could save 10 cents!

She was about to buy a package, when Trisha stopped her. "Don't buy it, Sam. You shouldn't eat all that sugar. And you can save more money by not buying any. Save your money for something better."

Try This

The next day Trisha went shopping with her mother. They were looking at small cartons of juice. An eight-ounce carton cost 50 cents. A six-ounce carton of the same brand cost 35 cents. Which was a better deal? Why?

Sharing the Apples

Trisha and her three friends went to the park with a picnic lunch. Trisha brought a bag of apples. She counted them—seven apples. How could they share seven apples fairly among four people?

Trisha said they could share the apples the way the ancient Egyptians might have done it 4,000 years ago. The Egyptians worked with unit fractions, which were fractions that had the numerator *one*.

First she gave each person one whole apple. Then she cut two of the remaining apples in half and gave each person a half apple. Finally, she cut the last apple into four equal parts, a quarter apple for each person. Each person has one plus a half plus a quarter: 1 + ½ + ¼ = 1¾ apples.

Jamal said he knew another way. Jamal always had bright ideas. "We can go to my house and make applesauce. Then we can give each person the same number of spoonfuls of applesauce."

Making Sense of the Cents

Samantha's Uncle Joe loved to pose riddles. Here are three of his riddles about money.

Riddle Number One

"I have 25 cents in pennies, nickels, and dimes. How many are there of each kind of coin if I have at least one of each?"

Samantha thought about it for a while. She got paper and pencil to write down all the possible combinations of pennies, nickels, and dimes. She did the arithmetic in her head. Here is some of her thinking:

- I know that the number of pennies must end in five or zero.
- What is the largest number of pennies? If I have one dime and one nickel, that makes 15 cents. I can have at most 10 pennies.
- What is the largest number of nickels? If I have one dime and five pennies, that is 15 cents. I can have at most 10 cents' worth of nickels, and that's two nickels.
- Can I have two dimes? That would leave only five cents. It won't work because I would have either five pennies or one nickel, not both.

How many?

She made a table that looked like this:

Pennies –1¢	Nickels –5¢	Dimes–10¢	Total
10 = 10¢	1 = 5¢	1 =10¢	25¢
5 = 5¢	2 =10¢	1 = 10¢	25¢

Samantha told Uncle Joe the two possible answers: 10 pennies, 1 nickel, 1 dime, or 5 pennies, 2 nickels, 1 dime.

"Good *number sense*!" said Uncle Joe. Then he gave her another money riddle.

Riddle Number Two

I have 40 coins in my piggy bank, all pennies and nickels. They add up to a dollar. How many pennies and how many nickels are in the bank?

Samantha thought about this problem for a while. Then she decided to make a table and list possible combinations of 40 pennies and nickels. Again, she knew that the number of pennies must end in five or zero. She could mark the combination that added up to a dollar.

Pennies	Nickels	Total Number	Total Value
40	0	40	40¢
35	5 = 25¢	40	60¢
30	10 = 50¢	40	80¢
25	15 = 75¢	40	100¢ = $1.00

The answer is 25 pennies and 15 nickels. She also noticed that the sum went up by 20¢ each time the number of nickels went up by five.

Uncle Joe was so proud of her that he gave her another money riddle, a more complicated one.

Riddle Number Three

How can 11 coins be combined to make one dollar, using any of the following coins: pennies, nickels, dimes, and quarters?

Samantha decided to work with the quarters, then figure out how many other coins she would need to make a dollar. She started with the easiest combination. This is the chart she set up:

Quarters 25¢	Dimes 10¢	Nickels 5¢	Pennies 1¢	Number of coins	Value in cents
3 = 75¢	1 = 10¢	2 = 10¢	5 = 5¢	11	100¢
3 = 75¢	1 = 10¢	1 = 5¢	10 = 10¢	15	100¢
3 = 75¢	0	3 = 15¢	5 = 5¢	11	95¢
2 = 50¢	2 = 20¢	2 = 10¢	5 = 5¢	11	85¢
2 = 50¢	3 = 30¢	6 = 30¢	0	11	110¢

The first combination was easy. Samantha first tried working with three quarters. She needed eight more coins to add up to 25¢. She looked back at the first riddle. There was the answer: one dime, two nickels, and five pennies, eight coins adding up to 25¢.

Then she tried other combinations with three quarters. She wrote down all the numbers that she tried, even if they turned out to be wrong. No other combination worked with three quarters.

Then she tried working with two quarters, or 50¢. She would need nine more coins to add up to another 50¢. Again, she wrote down all her trials.

She found two more combinations that worked. One combination that worked had two quarters but no pennies. The other had one quarter but no pennies.

Try This

1. Find the two combinations that worked for Samantha. One had two quarters and the other had one quarter, but no pennies in either combination.

2. Can you find any other combinations of the 11 coins that add up to a dollar?

3. Make up a coin riddle. Ask a friend to solve it.

Count the Change

When I was a little girl, my parents opened a clothing store. When I was about eight years old, they trusted me to work at the cash register. My father taught me to "count on." For example, a customer bought socks that cost 59 cents. She gave me a dollar. To give change, I said aloud: "59, 60, 65, 75, one dollar," as I picked up a penny, a nickel, a dime, and a quarter. Then I repeated the same words as I gave the customer her change, one coin at a time. Working in the store helped me to build my *number sense*.

Today the clerk in the supermarket doesn't have to think very much about the numbers. The computer tells her how much change to pick up. Of course, she still needs to count out the correct amount. Often she needs to know more than that, like when a customer complains about a mistake.

Try This

Next time you go shopping with an adult, look at the register tape. What information does it give you?

A Head for Numbers

You may have heard the remark, "She has a head for numbers." It means that she is good at working with numbers. She may be able to calculate easily in her head, to do mental arithmetic. She may know how to figure out an estimate, which is how to use an easy method to get an answer that's close to the exact answer. With practice,

anyone can have a head for numbers, a good *number sense*.

Having a head for numbers may help to save lives. A newspaper story (*New York Times*, August 29, 1987) tells about a tractor-trailer driver who was working with his calculator instead of looking at the road. He was trying to figure out his gas mileage, which is how many miles he drove for each gallon of gasoline. As a result, he rammed into a car, and that set off many more accidents. Six people were killed (but not the driver) and 13 were injured. You can imagine the condition of the cars!

Suppose the driver had gone 486 miles on 19 gallons of gasoline. He wanted to divide 19 into 486, but couldn't do that while he was driving. What he could do is round the two numbers so that he could do the division in his head. He could say, "Nineteen is close to 20, and 486 is close to 500. 500 divided by 20 is 25. I can drive about 25 miles on a gallon of gas."

Try This

Suppose the driver had gone 619 miles on 21.3 gallons of gasoline. Estimate his gas mileage, which is the number of miles he could drive on one gallon of gasoline. Do the work in your head.

Tom Fuller, the African Calculator

Thomas Fuller was brought to America as a slave in the year 1724, when he was 14 years old. Slaves were not allowed to learn to read or write or go to school. Fuller really had a head for numbers and wonderful *number sense*. He could multiply two large numbers in his head and get an exact answer. He could figure out how much seed to plant on the farm and how much wood was needed for a building. Perhaps his people in Africa were traders. African traders have been known for their great ability in mental calculations.

Abolitionists (people who were against slavery) spoke of the slave Fuller's superior mathematical abilities. For example, an abolitionist asked Fuller the age in *seconds* of a person who was 70 years, 17 days, and 12 hours of age. Fuller needed only one and a half minutes to figure out the answer: 2,210,500,800 seconds. Meanwhile, the man who asked the question was working it out with pencil and paper. When he gave a different answer, Fuller told him that he had forgotten about the leap years. Fuller had the right answer. Fuller earned the name "the African Calculator." He lived his life as a slave

on the farm of Mrs. Elizabeth Cox. She refused to sell him, even though she was offered large sums of money, because his great calculating skills were invaluable to her farm.

The Missing Dot

Samantha's mother opened the envelope and took out a bill. Then she laughed. "One thousand eight hundred ninety-five dollars for a book! What a mistake!"

She showed the bill to Samantha. "Sam, what do you think is wrong with this bill? It's for a book I ordered for your cousin Eddie for his birthday."

Samantha looked at the bill and saw the amount: $1895. "I think it should be eighteen dollars and ninety-five cents. Is that right?"

"Yes, that's correct. I'll call the store and ask them to correct the mistake."

She did that. Then she reported back to Samantha. "They said the computer made the mistake. Blame it on the computer. What *nonsense*! A computer has no *number sense*. It does only what a person tells it to do."

She crossed out $1895 and wrote $18.95. That little dot, the decimal point, made all the difference.

We use a decimal point to show dollars and cents:

- A dollar is worth one hundred cents: $1.00 = 100¢

- $0.25 = 25¢ = ¼ of a dollar (read "a quarter of a dollar").
- $0.05 = 5¢ = ¹⁄₂₀ of a dollar = 0.05 of a dollar (read "five-hundredths").
- $6.25 means six dollars and twenty-five cents. You can also read it as six and a quarter dollars, or six dollars and a quarter.
- $6.05 means six dollars and five cents.

Try This

1. Fill in the correct number in front of each sentence:

_____ half dollars equal one dollar.

_____ quarters equal one dollar.

_____ dimes equal one dollar.

_____ nickels equal one dollar.

_____ pennies equal one dollar.

2. Write the value of each coin—half dollar, quarter, dime, nickel, and penny—in three ways (follow the example above):

(a) With a dollar sign and a decimal point;
(b) with a cents sign;
(c) as a fraction of a dollar.

Number Sense and Common Sense

Sometimes you need more than *number sense* to get the right answer to a problem. You also need *common sense*. The answer may depend on the situation you are dealing with. Here are four examples. They all call for division of 100 by 40. But they'll have different answers.

1. Divide 100 by 40. The answer is 2, with a remainder of 20. The answer may also be given as $2^{20}/_{40}$, or $2\frac{1}{2}$, or 2.5.

2. One hundred people are going on a trip by bus. Each bus holds 40 people. How many buses are needed?

The answer "2½ buses" is *nonsense*. Can you picture 2½ buses? They would need 3 buses, although the buses might not be filled completely.

3. A bar of candy costs 40 cents. I have one dollar. How many bars of candy can I buy for a dollar?

The answer is *two* bars. The clerk will not sell a half bar of candy.

4. Forty students are putting on a musical. Each student will wear a ribbon. The teacher has 100 feet of ribbon to divide equally among the students. Find the length of each piece, to the nearest inch.

The answer is 2 feet and 6 inches, or 30 inches.

Try This

Think of a problem for which you must use *common sense* to get the right answer. Ask a friend to solve it.

Whose Foot?

Trisha's family bought a new rug for the living room. Her mother said it measured nine by twelve.

"Nine by twelve what?" asked Trisha. "Nine by twelve feet," her mother said.

Trisha decide to check it out. She walked along the shorter edge of the rug, heel to toe. She made sure that the back of one shoe touched the tip of the other shoe as she counted her steps.

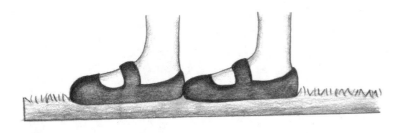

"Thirteen feet," she announced.

Her younger brother wanted to get into the act. He also walked along the edge of the rug and counted his steps. "I got 15 feet."

A long time ago people would measure things by using parts of their body. They might use their feet, their arms, their hands, or their fingers. In some parts of the world, they still measure that way. But whose foot, whose arm, whose hand should they use? Each person has a different measure.

Units of measure had to be *standardized*. A foot must be a specific length, no matter who measured it.

Now most of the world uses the metric system. This system is based on 10, like our number system. The meter measures length and the gram measures mass (or weight). A kilometer is 1,000 meters, and a kilogram is 1,000 grams. The word *kilo* comes from the Greek word for "thousand."

Of course, no measurement is ever *exact*!

Try This

Choose a room in your home. Measure the width of the room with your own feet as Trisha did. First *estimate* how many of your feet it measures. Write your answer on a piece of paper. After you have measured, see how close the actual measurement is to your estimate.

An Expensive Mistake

In September 1999 the Mars Orbiter was due to arrive at and go into orbit around the planet Mars. It was supposed to measure the climate on Mars. But the spacecraft never arrived. It was lost. What happened to it?

Finally the reason for the loss was made public. It was due to "a mix-up between English and metric units in the navigation data," according to the *New York Times* (December 8, 1999). People at the space agency, NASA, used metric units—meters and grams—in their plans. The engineers who built the spacecraft to these plans used feet and pounds, the English system. As a result, the spacecraft went off course and was destroyed.

The cost of this mistake was $125,000,000—125 million dollars of the taxpayers' money!

Try This

Look up the units of length in the metric system. How are they related to one another? Do the same in the "foot" system (English system) of length. Which system is easier to use?

Riddles, Puzzles, and Other Mind Bogglers

What's in This Chapter

Some people think math is just a big puzzle! In this chapter you will find riddles and puzzles, some silly, some tricky. You will learn tricks with numbers that will make even grown-ups wonder how you did them. You may want to start your own collection of riddles, puzzles, and number tricks.

Which Is Bigger?

"Which number is bigger, six-point-one or six-point-zero-nine?" Keisha asked her little sister Efua. Efua was just learning about dollars and cents. Keisha wrote the two numbers on a sheet of paper and showed them to Efua.

6.1 or 6.09

Efua looked at the two numbers for a while. "I don't know. I guess that one," she said, pointing to 6.09, "is bigger because nine is bigger than one."

"That fools you. Suppose you wanted six-point-one dollars," pointing to 6.1. "That's six and one-tenth dollars. A dime is a tenth of a dollar because 10 dimes make a dollar. A dime is 10 cents. The word *cents* means hundredths of a dollar, so a dime is 10 hundredths of a dollar. When it's about money, you write $6.10, and read it as six dollars and 10 cents."

"I can read six dollars and nine cents," Efua said proudly. "Oh, I get it. Ten cents is more money than nine cents. So $6.10 is bigger than $6.09."

"Right. Now you know that one-tenth is the same as ten-hundredths."

"But how do you read that number," she asked, pointing to 6.09, "when it's not about money? Gee, decimals are a puzzle!"

"You say six and nine-hundredths. One tenth, or ten-hundredths, is more than nine-hundredths."

Keisha thought this was a good riddle to try on other people. But why stop at one riddle? She decided to look in books and ask people for other riddles and puzzles about numbers. She could make up some herself. Keisha started a collection of number riddles and puzzles to share with her friends.

Some of her riddles were tricky. For example, how many months in the year have 30 days? (Answer: Eleven, all except February.)

Think About This

You might follow Keisha's example and make your own collection of riddles, puzzles, tricks, and games about numbers.

Keisha's Collection

1. Which expression has the larger answer:

   (a) 0 + 1 + 2 + 3 + 4 + 5
   (b) 0 × 1 × 2 × 3 × 4 × 5

2. Ed had 15 baseball cards. He gave away all but 10 cards. How many cards did he have left?

3. This riddle is a real oldie. Mr. Jackson raised rabbits and chickens. This collection of rabbits and chickens had 50 legs and 20 heads among them. How many rabbits and how many chickens did Mr. Jackson have?

4. Name the biggest number.

5. Reduce the fraction $6/8$.

6. Prove that half of 8 is 3. Then prove that half of 8 is 0.

7. Prove that half of 12 is seven.

8. Take 8 matchsticks and arrange them so that the sum is 13. Move one matchstick to another position so that the final answer is 130.

9. A merchant used a balance scale to weigh his products. He placed the items for sale in one pan of the balance scale. Then he placed the proper number of weights in the other pan until the two pans balanced. He found that with just four different weights, he could weigh any amount up to 15 pounds, to the nearest whole number of pounds. What are the weights?

   By adding another weight, he could weigh any amount up to 31 pounds. What is the additional weight?

10. Think of a number. Double it. Add 8. Find half of the sum. Subtract the original number. The answer should be 4.

    Now make up another riddle of this type.

11. *I am a huge, enormous number,*
    Seven digits, plain to see.
    But if you were to rub out one,
    Nothing would be left of me.
    What number am I?

12. Certain bacteria double in number every 10 minutes. In an experiment, the bacteria filled a dish at 4:30 P.M. At what time was the dish half full?

Guess My Number

Keisha wanted to include some number games and tricks in her collection. First she tried them out on Aviva. Aviva was helping to collect riddles for the collection.

"Aviva, let's play the 'Guess My Number' game. I want to see how it works out before I put it in my collection. Here are the rules:

- I write a number on a piece of paper, but I don't show it to you.
- You may ask me 10 questions about the number. I can answer only "yes" or "no."
- If you can't figure out my number after asking 10 questions, you give up, and I tell you the answer.

"I get it," said Aviva. "Let's play. Write a number."

Keisha wrote the number 68. These are the questions that Aviva asked, and Keisha's answers:

1. Is it even? Yes.

2. Is it more than 100? No.

3. Is it less than 50? No.

4. Is it more than 70? No. (Aviva now knows it is a number from 50 to 70.)

5. Is it a multiple of 10? No.

6. Is it a prime number? No. (This is a wasted question because Aviva was told that the number is even and more than 50.)

7. Is it a multiple of 4? Yes.

8. Is it more than 60? Yes.

9. Is it 64? No.

10. Is it 68? Yes, that's my number.

Aviva was able to guess on the 10th question.

Keisha was making tally marks to keep track of the number of questions. 卌 卌

The girls played the game again the next day. This time, three people took turns asking questions. They allowed 15 questions, so that each player had a chance to ask five questions, unless the game ended earlier.

Try This

When you play this game, make sure everyone knows the rules before the game starts. For example, the players might decide to use numbers less than 100. Decide how many questions will be allowed so that everyone has the same number of turns.

Liberian Stone Game

Keisha's teacher told her class about the Stone Game, played by children in Liberia, a country in Africa. Sixteen stones are arranged in two equal rows. One player goes out of the room, while the others decide which stone will be *it*. When the player returns to the room, he (or she) has to figure out which stone is *it*. He is allowed four questions, and the others can answer only with "yes" or "no." After each of the first three questions, he is allowed to interchange some of the stones between the two rows. If played correctly, he can figure out exactly which stone is *it*.

To get the hang of the game, Keisha, Eddie, and Aviva decide to play with eight objects, arranged in two rows. The "out" person will be allowed three questions. They use four circles and four squares, to help them remember which object is *it*. Here is how the game went. The objects are numbered to help keep track of them.

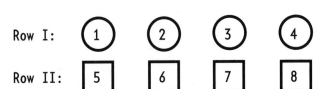

Row I: ① ② ③ ④

Row II: ⑤ ⑥ ⑦ ⑧

Figure 1

Aviva went out of the room. Keisha and Eddie decided that square 5 was *it*.

When Aviva returned, these were her questions and the answers:

1. Is it in Row I? No. Then Aviva interchanged the four odd-numbers objects.

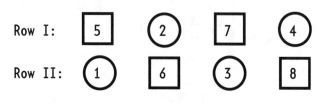

Row I: [5] (2) [7] (4)

Row II: (1) [6] (3) [8]

Figure 2

2. Is it in Row I? Yes. So then Aviva knew it must be 5 or 7. She interchanged two objects, 5 and 1. She did not move 2 or 4, because they had been in the first row at the beginning and she knew they were not *it*.

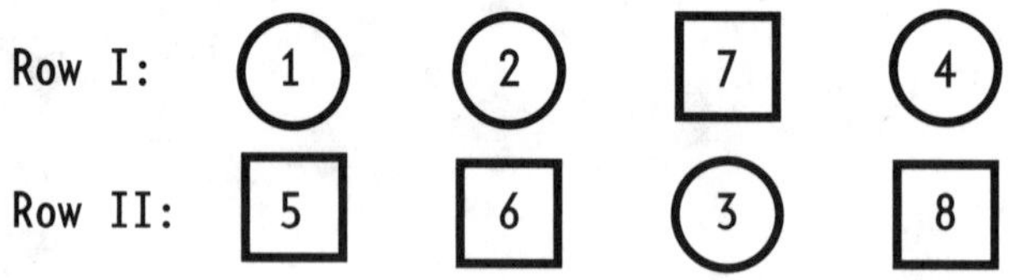

Row I: (1) (2) [7] (4)

Row II: [5] [6] (3) [8]

Figure 3

3. Is it in Row I? No. Then Aviva knew that 5 was *it*.

The trick is to interchange half the objects the first time and half of those the second time. Then continue interchanging half the previous number.

Try This

After you have played with eight pieces and three questions, try to play with 16 pieces and four questions, like the children in Liberia.

Guess the Digit

Aviva learned this trick from her brother Ben and told Keisha about it. She gave Keisha a pencil and paper and told her what to do.

1. Write a two-digit number, but don't show it to me.

2. Then write the same digits in the opposite order.

3. Subtract the smaller two-digit number from the larger number.

4. Draw a circle around one digit of the answer.

5. Tell me the other digit. Then I will tell you the circled digit.

   Keisha followed the directions. She wrote 52. Then she wrote 25. 52 minus 25 = 27. She circled the 2 in 27.

$$52; \quad 25; \quad 52-25 = \textcircled{2}7$$

She told Aviva that one digit was 7. Immediately Aviva announced that the other digit was 2.

Try This

Figure out how Aviva knew the second digit. Make up several examples and analyze them. Sometimes the answer has only one digit, for example:

$$65 - 56 = 9$$

Then the other digit must be zero.

Guess Two Digits

Aviva's brother Ben knew another trick like "Guess the Digit." Aviva asked Keisha to do the following:

1. Write a three-digit number, but don't show it.

2. Reverse the three digits; that is, write them in the opposite order.

3. Subtract the smaller number from the larger number.

4. Circle the hundreds digit and the tens digit in the answer.

5. Tell the number in the ones place. Aviva would then announce the two digits in the hundreds and tens places.

Keisha wrote 921. She reversed the digits and wrote 129. She subtracted:

$$921; \ 129; \ 921-129 = \textcircled{79}2$$

She drew a circle around 79 in the answer, and told Aviva that the ones digit was 2. Aviva knew that the other two digits were 7 and 9. How did she know?

Keisha had a bright idea. They could dress up the trick and put on a performance for their friends. Everyone would think they were geniuses!

They noticed that their telephone directory had 456 pages of listings. They would ask a volunteer to choose a three-digit number, reverse the digits, subtract the smaller number from the larger, and read the answer. Either Keisha or Aviva would then announce the first name on the page of the telephone directory without looking at the book. Of course, any number greater than 456 wouldn't count.

How many names did the girls have to memorize?

Try This

Play the game by yourself. Try several different examples until you discover the pattern. Then play the trick on your friends.

A Calendar Trick

It was June 30. Aviva tore off the page for June on her calendar and was about to throw it away.

Keisha stopped her. "Don't throw it away. I know a good trick with the calendar. I'll give you the directions:

"Draw a square around a three-by-three arrangement of numbers on the calendar. Show me the square. In a few seconds I will tell you the sum of all nine numbers in that square."

Aviva drew a square on the calendar page:

J U N E

1	2	3	4	5	6	7
8	9	10	11	12	13	14
15	16	17	18	19	20	21
22	23	24	25	26	27	18
29	30					

Keisha looked at the page. In no time at all she said, "The sum is 90."

Try This

1. Figure out how Keisha arrived at the sum so quickly. Did she add all the numbers in the square, or did she know a shortcut? Try the trick with several different squares on the calendar page. (Hint: Look at the middle number in the square.)

2. Look for other patterns in the calendar square. For example, draw the four lines that go through the middle number in the square: one horizontal line, one vertical line, and two diagonal lines. Add the three numbers that lie on each line. What do you discover?

Calendar Magic Square

Just as Aviva and Keisha were getting ready to throw away the calendar page, Aviva's brother Ben came into the room. He told the girls he knew another trick with the calendar square.

The trick was to rearrange the nine numbers in the square to form a magic square. In a magic square, the sum of the three numbers in each row, in each column, and in each diagonal is the same number, called the magic number.

Ben looked at the numbers in Aviva's square:

2	3	4
9	10	11
16	17	18

Ben drew another square on a sheet of paper. The magic number for a magic square is three times the center number. For this square the magic number is 3 × 10 = 30.

- In the center he placed the same center number, 10.
- Then he placed the odd numbers in the corners so that the three numbers in each diagonal had the magic sum of 30, or 3 × 10.
- He placed the four remaining numbers so that the magic sum was 30 for each row and each column.

Here is his magic square. Check it out.

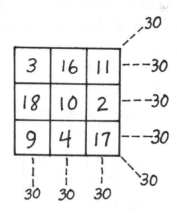

Try This

Draw a square around a three-by-three array of numbers on a calendar page. Rearrange the numbers to form a magic square.

Here is a hint: If the center number is even, place the odd numbers in the corners of the square. If the center number is odd, place the even numbers in the corners. What is the reason?

The Monkey's Age

Keisha put into her collection this *nonsense* riddle, to make people laugh. She didn't expect anyone to solve it.

The monkey's mother is one-half as old as the monkey will be when it is three times as old as its mother was when she was one-half as old as the monkey will be when it is as old as its mother will be when she is four times as old as the monkey was when it was twice as old as its mother was when she was one-third as old as the monkey was when it was as old as its mother was when she was three times as old as the monkey was when it was one-fourth as old as it is now. The combined ages of the monkey and its mother are 30 years. How old is the monkey?

Fingers, Words, Sticks, Strings, and Symbols

What's in This Chapter

Numbers are all around us. Can you imagine a world without numbers? Your age, your birthday, the cost of a book or toy—all are expressed in numbers.

How did numbers begin? That's hard to know. Did people have *words* for numbers before they *wrote* numbers? Probably they used their fingers and other parts of their bodies to show how many and how much.

This chapter is a short history of numbers. We'll start with marks on a bone, made many thousands of years ago. Then we'll describe how and why some people used their fingers for counting. You will learn the finger signs for the num-

bers 1 to 10 used by the Plains Indians of North America, invented long before there was a United States. Then you will learn some of the number words of people who speak the Spanish, Yup'ik (Eskimo), Mayan, and Igbo languages. Their number systems grew from finger counting, and in some cases, from finger-and-toe counting. After learning something about their number systems, you will figure out their names for larger numbers.

People needed to write numbers. You will learn about several systems of numerals, some more than 5,000 years old. Nowadays, many people in the world use the Indo-Arabic system that is familiar to you.

Notches on a Bone

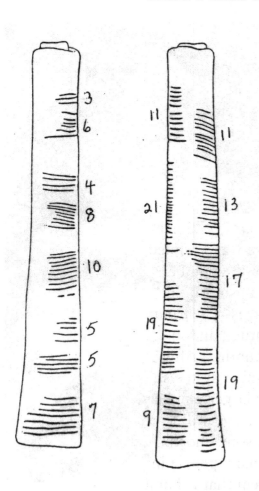

About 50 years ago, a Belgian scientist digging near the village of Ishango, in Congo, Africa, found a small bone covered with notches. Attached to one end of the bone was a bit of quartz that may have been used to make the marks. The illustration shows two sides of the bone.

The scientist, Dr. Jean de Heinzelin, counted the marks. He thought that one side showed numbers and their doubles, and the other side showed prime numbers. Another scientist, Alexander Marshack, looked at the bone under a microscope. He decided that the marks were the record of a six-month calendar based on the cycles of the moon.

At first the bone was dated to about 9,000 years ago. Later, using better scientific methods of dating, they found that the bone might be as old as 25,000 years!

This bone, called the Ishango bone, is now famous. But we can never know exactly how this bone was used so long ago. Examine the drawings carefully. What evidence do you find for each theory? A cycle of the moon, called a lunar cycle, is about 29½ days in length. Which theory makes more *number sense* to you? Perhaps the notches on the bone have nothing to do with numbers, after all! What do you think?

Long before the invention of written numbers, people made marks on bones or sticks to keep track of things. We still make such marks, usually on paper. People playing a game may make marks like these to keep score:

The score is 10. Each group has five strokes called "tally marks." Guess why the marks are in groups of five. The next section will give you a hint.

How Many Fingers?

Imagine that you are in a market in a faraway land. You see a pyramid of beautiful big round oranges. Mmm, wouldn't an orange taste good! Suppose that you decide to buy four oranges.

You tell the market woman that you want four oranges. But she doesn't know your language. All the people around you speak a language that you don't understand. What can you do? You can point to the oranges and show four on your fingers. How would you do that?

You can probably think of a lot of ways to use your fingers to show four. You might raise four fingers, or bend them, or move your fingers some other way. You might use four fingers on one hand, either the right hand or the left hand. Or you might use both hands to show four; for example, three fingers on the right hand and one finger on the left hand.

If you decide to raise your fingers, which four fingers will you raise? Some ways are awkward or hard to do. Besides, you might want to use just one hand so that your other hand is free to carry a bundle or to point to something. Try out some ways and see which ways are easiest. You might choose just one or two ways that make the most sense to you.

Native American Number Signs

Some people have special ways of using their fingers to count. When people who speak different languages come together, they may invent a sign language that is understood by all the groups present. That is what happened hundreds of years ago when many tribes of Native Americans lived on the Great Plains. On the next page are their signs for the numbers from 1 to 10.

To show four, they raised four fingers, but not the thumb, on the right hand. Doesn't that method show good *number sense*?

Other people have developed different ways that make sense to them. The Zulu people of South Africa raise four fingers, but not the thumb, on the left hand. Probably all people use just one hand to show four.

People who use their fingers to count can *feel* the numbers without having to count their fingers. They have developed *number sense* in their fingers.

Try This

Make up your own system of finger signs for numbers. Draw them on paper and try them out on a friend.

Think About This

Can you believe that there are 210 different ways to raise four fingers?

- There are five different ways to raise four fingers on the right hand. It might be easier to think about the one finger that you will not raise.
- There are five different ways to raise four fingers on the left hand.
- There are 200 ways to raise four fingers, using both hands together.

See how many of these ways you can discover. Keep a list so that you don't repeat the different ways. You might number the fingers from 1 to 10 and make a chart of the fingers you raise for each method.

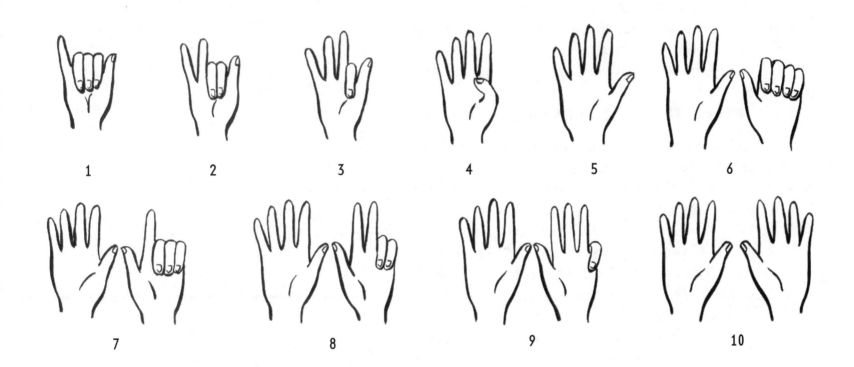

1 2 3 4 5 6

7 8 9 10

Names for Numbers: Base Ten

Imagine that you are making up a new language. You have to make up names for the numbers from 1 to 100. Would it make sense to invent a hundred different unconnected words? Or would it make more *number sense* to invent a *system* in which the words are connected to one another?

Number Words in English

Think about the meanings of the words *fourteen* and *forty*. *Fourteen* is a short way of saying "four plus ten." The words that end in "teen" tell you to *add ten* to three, four, and so on, up to nine. Why do we say "twenty" not "tenteen"?

Forty is a short way of saying "four times ten." The number words that end in "ty" tell you to *multiply 10* times two, three, four, up to nine. Why do we say "hundred," not "tenty"?

You might wonder about the words *eleven* and *twelve*. *Eleven* means "one left" after counting the ten fingers, and *twelve* means "two left" after ten fingers have been counted. So you see that many people counted on their fingers. In some languages the word for "hand" also means "five."

The English system of number words is based on tens. So is the Spanish system that you will read about next. Why is ten such an important number? Just count your fingers to find the answer!

Number Words in Spanish

Spanish	English	Spanish	English
uno	one	once	eleven
dos	two	diez y seis	sixteen
tres	three	diez y nueve	nineteen
cuatro	four	treinta	thirty
cinco	five	setenta y dos	seventy-two
seis	six	noventa y nueve	ninety-nine
siete	seven		
ocho	eight		
nueve	nine		
diez	ten		

Try This

Study the Spanish number words and figure out the system. Then give the English words for each of the Spanish number words below:

diez y siete

trece

cuarenta y cuatro

diecisiete

cincuenta

diez y ocho

catorce

sesenta y cinco

Names for Numbers: Base Twenty

Some people counted their fingers and toes. For them, *twenty* was the most important number in their system. The word for twenty means "a whole person" in some languages. The English word *score* means twenty, as in the famous words of President Abraham Lincoln, spoken in 1863:

Four score and seven years ago our fathers brought forth on this continent a new nation, conceived in liberty, and dedicated to the proposition that all men are created equal.

Today he might have said "all men and women are created equal." At the time of his speech, women and slaves did not have many of the rights of white men, such as the right to vote or to own property.

What happened four score and seven years before 1863?

Number Systems That Group by Twenties

Long before Columbus sailed to America, the Maya and other people were living in southern Mexico and northern Central America. Millions of their descendents live there today. The Yup'ik Eskimos live in western Alaska. Igbo people live in eastern Nigeria, a country in West Africa. Grouping quantities by twenties makes *number sense* to all these different peoples.

English	Maya (Yucatec)	Yup'ik	Igbo
one	hun	atauciq	otu
two	ca	malruk	abuo
three	ox	pingayun	ato
four	can	cetaman	ano
ten	lahun	qula	iri
twenty	hun kal	yuinaq	ohu
forty	ca kal	yuinaak malruk	ohu abuo

Try This

1. Figure out what these names mean and write them in English. Try these:

Maya:	lahun kal	can kal
Yup'ik:	yuinaat cetaman	yuinaat pingayun
Igbo:	ohu iri	ohu ato

2. Write each number as groups of twenties plus a number less than twenty:

Example: 94 = 4 × 20 + 14

146 = ____   235 = ____   399 = ____

Think About This

The Igbo word for "four hundred" is *nnu*. Why do you think they have a separate word for this number? (Hint: Think of the English word "hundred.")

Our Indo-Arabic Numerals

People also needed to write numbers. Today many people around the world use the Indo-Arabic (also called Hindu-Arabic, or Arabic) numerals—0, 1, 2, 3, 4, 5, 6, 7, 8, 9—that are familiar to you. They were invented in India at least 14 centuries ago. The system was spread by the Arabs to other parts of Asia, to north Africa, and to southern Europe. It was not until centuries later that the system became widespread in Europe and began to replace Roman numerals.

People called the new numerals "Arabic." At first, people were afraid to use them. A merchant would think: "Suppose someone tries to cheat me by changing a 1 to a 7! Those Arabic numbers make *no sense*." In fact, the city of Florence passed a law against the use of these numerals. Later, people realized how easy they were to work with. Indo-Arabic numerals became popular in Europe about 400 years ago.

When you learn about other systems of numerals, you will see the convenience of our Indo-Arabic system. Here are some reasons:

- It has just ten different symbols, called *digits*. Our fingers and toes are called "digits." Why are the number symbols also called "digits"?
- It has a symbol for zero.
- It has place value, or positional notation. For example, the numeral 340 is different from 304 or 430 or 403, even though all these numerals have the same three digits. The value of the number depends on the position of each digit.
- You can write any number, no matter how large or how small.
- It is easy to do arithmetic using this numeral system.

You will compare Indo-Arabic numerals with the number signs invented in ancient times in Egypt, China, and Rome, by the Maya and other people of Mexico and Central America, and by the Inca of the South American Andes.

Numbers in Stone in Ancient Egypt

Over 5,000 years ago, people in northern Africa and western Asia began to build cities and trade with one another. They needed to write numbers in order to keep track of business and make records of taxes. The people of Egypt and Sumer (also called Mesopotamia, now Iraq) developed *systems* of number signs, called numerals. The two systems were very different from each other. Here you will learn about the Egyptian system.

Egypt is in northeast Africa. It became a powerful country over 5,000 years ago. Large pyramids and temples were built for the king, whom they called the pharaoh (FAIR-oh). On the walls, workers carved stories about the pharaoh and great events, using symbols for their words and numbers called hieroglyphs (hy-roh-GLIFS).

The Egyptians had a different form of writing on papyrus, an early type of paper. For this writing they had a system of number symbols that are more like those we use today.

Here are some examples of Egyptian numbers in stone and their meanings:

3　　　40　　　39

Try This

1. Figure out the meaning of each symbol. Then write these Egyptian numerals our way, in Indo-Arabic numerals:

I	∩	II∩	III∩∩	III ∩∩∩∩	I ∩∩∩∩ ∩∩∩∩

2. Compare the numerals:

 and 98

Which is easier to write, Egyptian hieroglyphs or Indo-Arabic numerals? Which is easier to understand?

3. This is the number 1,238 in hieroglyphs.

⦙⦙⦙⦙ ∩∩∩ 99 ⌐

Figure out the meaning of each symbol. Then translate each Egyptian numeral into an Indo-Arabic numeral:

⫼∩ 999/999   ∩∩∩/∩∩ 99   ⦙⦙⦙ 999 ⌐   ∩∩ ⌐⌐⌐/⌐⌐⌐

Think About This

1. Write a story about ancient Egypt that has at least four different numbers. Write the numbers the Egyptian way.

2. Compare the two systems: Egyptian hieroglyphic numbers and Indo-Arabic numerals. How are they alike? How are they different? If you mixed up the Egyptian symbols for the number 1,238, could you still read the number? Which way of writing makes more *number sense* to you?

3. Look up the Mesopotamian system of numeration. It is based on grouping numbers by tens and sixties. That's why we have sixty minutes in an hour and sixty seconds in a minute.

Chinese Stick Numerals

Chinese stick numerals, also called *rod numerals*, were in use at least 2,000 years ago. They were used for calculations. The rods were placed on a counting board with columns for the ones, the tens, the hundreds, and so on. People moved the sticks to add and subtract numbers.

Here are some Chinese numerals, with their values shown using our numerals.

Some are missing. Figure out the pattern.

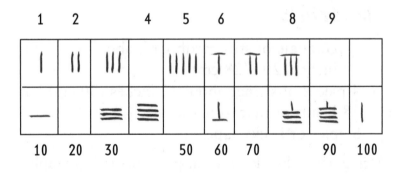

1	2		4	5	6		8	9	
│	║	║│		║║│	┰	┰┰	┰┰┰		
─		═	≡		⊥		⊥	⊥	│
10	20	30		50	60	70		90	100

Figure 1

Try This

1. Fill in the missing numbers in Figure 9.

2. This is a drawing of a Chinese counting board.

	1000	100	10	1
8,604	⊥ / ═	┰		║║║
───		║║║	═	┰
───		═	┰┰┰	─

The first number is 8,604. What are the second and third numbers?

Think About This

Compare the Chinese rod system with the Indo-Arabic system. How are they the same? How are they different? Which system makes more *number sense* to you?

The Chinese Abacus

Chinese stick numerals were used on a counting board. Later, when the Chinese invented paper, they wrote the same symbols on paper. Instead of an empty column to represent zero, they borrowed the zero symbol from India. They still used the counting board for calculations like adding and subtracting.

Someone in China had the bright idea for a more convenient counting board. Beads were strung on cords and attached to a frame. The

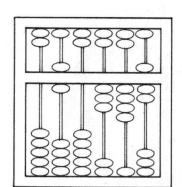

Chinese called this device a *suan pan*, which means "counting board." We call it an *abacus*. You may have seen an abacus in Chinese shops or restaurants. It lies flat on a table. This abacus shows the number 60,347.

The cords have place value—units, tens, hundreds—just like in our system. The five beads below the crossbar are units. The two beads above the crossbar represent fives. Figure out how the number 60,347 is represented.

People who learn to use an abacus develop *number sense* in their fingers and their brains. They do some of the calculations in their heads. They can work very fast.

Try This

1. Read the number shown on each drawing of the *suan pan*.

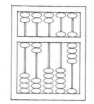 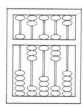

2. Make a *suan pan* having four cords.

.Materials

A rectangle of stiff cardboard, about 8½ × 11 inches (20 × 28 cm)
4 pieces of string, about 12 inches (30 cm) long
28 beads or macaroni pieces
Stapler or sticky tape

String seven beads on each piece of string. Staple or tape each strand to the cardboard in three places. Then figure out how to use the abacus for adding and subtracting.

Think About This

The *suan pan* is like using the fingers of one or two hands, grouping by fives and tens. How does it relate to Chinese stick numerals?

Roman Numerals: Old and New

Like most people, Benita has II eyes, XX fingers and toes, and CCVI bones. She was born in the year MDCCCCLXXXVIIII. Her mother's age is XXXXIIII years.

The Romans used letters of their alphabet to represent numbers. You probably know some of them already. Here they are:

I = 1 V = 5 X = 10 L = 50 C = 100
D = 500 M = 1,000

Translate all five Roman numerals in the paragraph about Benita into Indo-Arabic numerals. Then figure out Benita's age.

The Roman numerals in the story about Benita may look strange, but that is how the Romans wrote them over 2,000 years ago. Centuries later people said: "It makes *no sense* to repeat all those symbols. Let's use subtraction to show one unit less than the symbol that follows. For example, instead of writing VIIII, let's save time and write IX." Here is the story about Benita, written the modern way:

Like most people, Benita has II eyes, XX fingers and toes, and CCVI bones. She was born in the year MCMLXXXIX. Her mother's age is XLIV years.

Which method of writing Roman numerals makes more *number sense* to you?

The Romans didn't add and multiply with numerals, the way we do. Instead, they used a counting board for their calculations.

Try This

Using Roman numerals, multiply CCXXXIV by LXXVIII. Not easy!

The Inca Quipu: Knots on a String

From about the year 1400 to 1540, the Inca (also spelled Inka) ruled a tremendous area along the mountains and deserts of the western coast of South America. Cuzco, the capital city, was two miles above sea level in the country now called Peru. The people they ruled spoke many languages. How did the government keep track of everything?

They used *quipus* to keep records. A *quipu* is a collection of colored strings in which knots have been tied to show various numbers. The color of the string and the way it was placed gave the key to the meaning of each quantity. Messengers running in relays carried the quipus from the towns and villages to the capital city Cuzco. These quipus told the quantities of food in storage, amount of taxes collected, and much other information.

You can figure out the code of the quipu. Study the example in Figure 2.

The small circles are knots. Each string has knots showing a different number in a system based on the number ten.

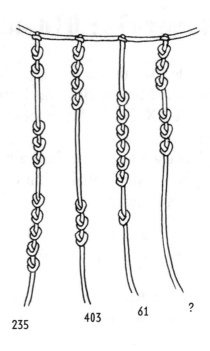

235   403   61   ?

Figure 2

Try This

1. Figure out the system. What number is shown on the fourth string?

2. You can draw your own quipu. You will need three pencils of different colors and a sheet of paper. You may want to use a ruler.

Draw three strings of different colors tied to a main string. Draw knots to show these three numbers: 172, 45, and 230.

The Bars and Dots of the Maya

For thousands of years the Maya have lived in southern Mexico and Central America, where they built great temples and large cities. Their scientists knew a great deal about the stars and planets, kept track of time for millennia (thousands of years), and were able to calculate with large numbers. Using place value and just three symbols—bar, dot, and zero symbol—they could write numbers in the millions.

When people traded in the marketplace, they laid sticks and pebbles on the ground to show numbers, with a shell to represent zero. It made *number sense* to use the same kind of symbols for writing numbers—bars to stand for sticks, and dots to represent pebbles.

Here are some of the Maya symbols and their values shown using our numerals.

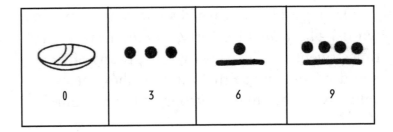

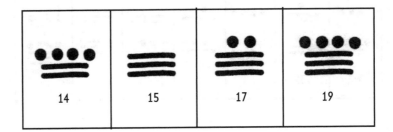

See whether you can crack the code.

- What does the dot stand for?
- What does the bar stand for?
- How did they write zero?

On page 83 you learned some Mayan number words. The words for forty, *ca kal*, means "two times twenty." The Maya wrote groups of bars and dots, one *above* the other, to show place value, with the smallest group at the bottom.

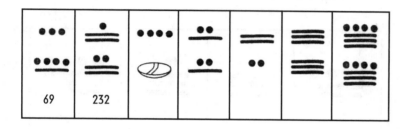

Try This

Study the examples on this page. Note how the bars, dots, and zero symbol are placed. The group having the lowest value is at the bottom. Then write the value of the Mayan number, using our numerals, in the five remaining examples above.

Think About This

What is the largest number that can be written in the bottom group? What is the largest number that can be written with two groups?

The Calculator and Number Sense

What's in This Chapter

Tom had a new calculator. "Now I don't need to know all those number facts," he said to his friend Kazu. "I'll just let the calculator do all the work."

"But you still need to be able to work with numbers," she replied. "How would you know if you pressed the wrong key?"

"I guess you're right. My mother told me that a clerk at the supermarket checkout pressed $5.19 instead of $1.59. My mother was estimating the bill in her head and caught the mistake right away."

A calculator is a wonderful little tool. It can add and subtract. It can do multiplication and division computations. Many calculators can do

other kinds of arithmetic. And it does these things quickly and accurately.

In this chapter you will use your calculator to discover some interesting patterns of numbers. You can also find these patterns by doing pencil and paper arithmetic, but the calculator will do the work for you more quickly. That gives you more time to figure out the patterns.

You will also learn some calculator games to play alone or with friends, and tricks to play on your friends.

The calculator is very handy, but it has no *number sense*. The person who operates the calculator still needs number sense to know what keys to press and how to use the numbers.

A New Kind of Number

Tom enjoyed experimenting with his calculator. "Let's see what happens when I subtract seven from four."

Kazu objected. "You can't subtract a bigger number from a smaller number."

Meanwhile Tom was pressing the keys:

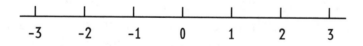

The answer was −3. Read this number "negative three." Some people say "minus three." Tom had discovered negative numbers.

What are negative numbers? On the number line they are the numbers to the left of zero.

```
  |    |    |    |    |    |    |
 -3   -2   -1    0    1    2    3
```

The numbers to the right of zero are called positive numbers. There is an infinite number of negative numbers and of positive numbers.

What are negative numbers good for? You probably know some uses already.

- When the temperature goes down below zero, the reading is a negative number. The temperature is 10 degrees below zero, or negative 10 degrees.

- A loss of five yards on the football field can be thought of as negative five yards.
- The years before the first year on our calendar are negative numbers. We say "in the year 240 B.C.E.," meaning 240 years before the Common Era. We also say "in the year 240 B.C.," meaning 240 years before Christ.
- When the ancient Egyptians built the pyramids, about 4,600 years ago, they drew lines to measure distance above ground (positive) and distance below ground (negative).

Try This

Find more uses for negative numbers. Ask your friends and family to help you in your search.

Calculator Games for Two or More

"Let's play a calculator game," suggested Tom. "We set the calculator at zero. Then we take turns adding one, two, or three to the sum. The person to get a sum of exactly 20 is the winner."

Kazu and Tom played the game twice. Tom won the first game and Kazu won the second. They were starting to become bored. Then Kazu said she had a good idea.

"Let's start at 20 and subtract one, two, or three each time. The person who reaches zero is the winner."

Along came Ron. He wanted to play, too. Three people could take turns. They decided to start at zero and add any number from one to five until one person reached exactly 100.

Then they began to think of other variations. Suppose that they were not allowed to add or subtract a one. Would that make winning the game impossible?

Try This

1. Play the games that Tom and his friends played.

2. Play the calculator game without using the number one. For example, set the calculator display at zero. Take turns adding any number from two to nine until one person reaches exactly 100.

3. Make up some new calculator games. You can try them out by playing the games by yourself.

More Calculator Games

After playing several calculator games, Tom and Kazu decided to make up a different type of game for the calculator. They pretended that some of the calculator keys were broken. How could they use the remaining keys to get a certain number? Here are some of the games they invented.

Game 1

Suppose you need to show the number 24 on the display, but the 2 and the 4 keys are broken. Kazu and Tom thought of these number combinations:

$$19 + 5$$
$$37 - 13$$
$$8 + 8 + 8$$
$$3 \times 8$$
$$3 + 5 + 7 + 9$$
$$3 \times 10 - 6$$

Game 2

Suppose you want to show the three-digit number 345 on the display, but the 3, 4, and 5 keys are broken. Tom and Kazu thought of these combinations of numbers:

$$126 + 219$$
$$127 + 218$$
$$128 + 217$$
$$129 + 216$$
$$611 - 266$$
$$612 - 267$$
$$612 - 266 - 1$$
$$612 - 167 - 100$$
$$226 + 109 + 10$$
$$226 + 108 + 11$$
$$226 + 107 + 12$$

Try This

1. Look at the number combinations in Game 2. What patterns do you find?

2. Make up more number combinations for the two games that Kazu and Tom played.

3. Make up other games of the same type. Play them by yourself or with a friend.

What Comes First?

Kazu had a fancy calculator. It had a lot of keys. Her mother bought an even fancier calculator and gave her old one to Kazu.

"Let's see which calculator is faster," she said to Tom. "Let's do this problem." She wrote:

$$236 + 528 \times 4 =$$

They both started at the same time. Tom called out "3,056" just as Kazu said "2,348."

"One of us, maybe both of us, made a mistake," said Tom. "Let's do it again." Their answers were the same as before.

What was wrong? Why did they get two different answers to the same problem?

They decided to do an easier calculation with the addition and multiplication keys, a calculation that they could do mentally at the same time:

$$6 + 5 \times 2$$

Again they got two different answers. Kazu's calculator display showed 16, while Tom's showed 22. It made no sense. It was *nonsense*!

Finally they figured out the answer to the puzzle. Tom's calculator did:

$$6 + 5 = 11, \text{ then } 11 \times 2 = 22$$

Kazu's calculator did:

$$5 \times 2 = 10, \text{ then } 6 + 10 = 16$$

Why the difference?

Here is the correct answer, which follows the rule called the *Order of Operations*. This is the rule:

Multiplication and division come before addition and subtraction.

Look again at $6 + 5 \times 2$. If you want to add 6 and 5 first, you write

$$(6 + 5) \times 2$$

If you want to multiply 5×2 first, you write

$$6 + (5 \times 2), \text{ or just plain } 6 + 5 \times 2$$

Kazu's fancy calculator was designed to know that multiplication comes before addition. Tom's simple calculator just did the operations from left to right.

To do the multiplication first, Tom would have to press the calculator buttons in this order:

$$5 \times 2 + 6 =$$
$$or\ 5 \times 2 = + 6 =$$

Try This

1. Test your calculator with the problems that Kazu and Tom did. Does it operate like Tom's calculator or like Kazu's calculator?

2. Make up some problems that have both addition and multiplication and see which your calculator does first. Then include subtraction and division in your problems. Use numbers that are easy to work with. Do the work mentally as a check on your calculator.

A Number Trick

Ron greeted Kazu and Tom with a smile. "I know a good number trick. You can do it on the calculator. Tom, you write down a three-digit number and show it to Kazu. Hold on to the paper. Don't tell me the number."

Tom wrote 537 on a slip of paper and showed it to Kazu.

Ron continued: "Kazu, put that number in your calculator display. Then put it in again, so that you have a six-digit number in the display."

Kazu did what Ron told her to. The display showed:

537537

"Now, Kazu, divide that number by 7. Leave the answer in the display, but don't tell us what it is. Then divide that number by 11, and leave the answer in the display. Then divide that number by 13."

Kazu carried out the operations and looked to Ron for the next step.

"Show Tom the answer in your display."

Tom looked at the display and at the number on his paper. They were the same—537 in both places!

Try This

Do the trick with a different three-digit number. Why does it work? [Hint: Find the product of 7 x 11 x 13. Multiply the three-digit number by this product.]

Number Patterns

Cycle of Digits

Start with the number 142,857. (In a later section of this chapter you will learn why this number is important.)

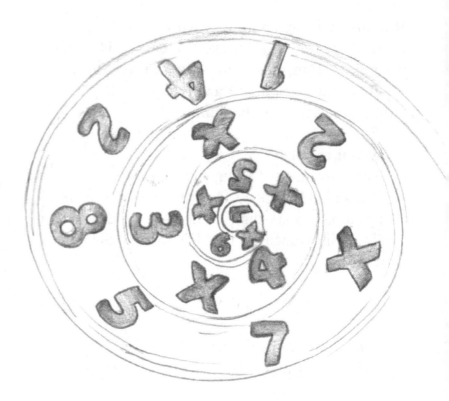

- Look at the digits in pairs. The first pair is 14. The second pair is 28. How are these two numbers related? The third pair is 57. How is 57 related to 28?
- Multiply 142,857 by 2 and write the answer on paper. (Note: Instead of using the multiplication key, you can do repeated addition.) How are the digits in the product related to the digits in the original number? How are the pairs of digits related?
- Multiply 142,857 by 3 and notice the pattern in the product.
- Multiply 142,857 by 4, then by 5, then by 6. Notice the patterns in the products.
- Multiply 142,857 by 7. What is your answer?

Try This

You can impress your friends with your ability to multiply in your head. Just memorize the number 142,857 and the first digit of each product. Tell your friends you can multiply that number by any number from two to seven without having to write anything down. Meanwhile, they can check your work by multiplying with paper and pencil or on a calculator.

Patterns with Nine

In this game you will multiply a number by 9 and find the digital of your answer. You find the digital by adding all the digits in the number. If the sum has more than one digit, add those digits. Keep doing this until the final answer has only one digit. That number is the digital of the product.

Suppose you choose 896. Place it in your calculator display. Multiply that number by 9.

896 × 9 = 8064. Find the digital of 8064.
8 + 0 + 6 + 4 = 18
1 + 8 = 9. The digital is 9.

Try This

1. Place any number in the display. Multiply it by 9. The digital of the answer should be 9. This can help you to memorize the multiplication facts for 9. It is also one way to check on your multiplication of any number by 9 (but this check doesn't *always* work, so be careful).
2. Multiply any number by a multiple of 9; for example, by 27 or by 99. What is the digital of the product?

Different Names for the Same Number

Tom was having so much fun experimenting with his calculator that his little brother Kenny wanted to share in the fun. Tom gave him the calculator and let him press the keys.

Tom decided to show him some tricks. "Look, I will put in different numbers, and get the same answer each time."

Here are some of the numbers he keyed in:

$$1 \div 2 = 0.5$$
$$2 \div 4 = 0.5$$
$$3 \div 6 = 0.5$$

Kenny thought Tom was very smart. Of course, what Tom was doing was changing the same common fraction in different forms to a decimal fraction. ½, ²⁄₄, ³⁄₆, and 0.5 are just different names for the same number. Some other names for ½ are: ⁵⁄₁₀, ⁵⁰⁄₁₀₀, 0.500, 50%, ¹⁶⁄₃₂, ¹⁰⁰⁰⁄₂₀₀₀, and many more. There is an infinite number of names for ½.

Try This

1. Write the fraction ¼ with as many different names as you can think of. Be sure to include decimal fractions and percent.

2. Do the same with 0.2 and with ¾. Then try other fractions.

Making Sense of Cents

Tom liked to add up the bill on his calculator when he went shopping with his family. One day their mother bought Kenny a toy car for $1.25 and bubble gum for five cents. This time Kenny wanted to add the bill.

Tom showed him how to key in 1.25, the number on the price tag. Then he pushed the addition key.

"I can do five cents myself," Kenny said. He keyed in .5 and =, giving the sum:

$$1.25 + .5 = 1.75$$

Kenny had keyed in .5. That's the same amount of money as $0.50, also written 50¢.

"That's too much money," Tom told his brother. "This is how you key in five cents." Tom keyed in:

$$1.25 + .05 = 1.30.$$

The bill was $1.30; one dollar and thirty cents.

Tom knew that the word *cent* means "one-hundredth of a dollar." So five cents is five-hundredths of a dollar, or $0.05.

"Wait a minute," he exclaimed. "I just caught on. Five cents is like five percent of a dollar. Cents, percent—both words mean 'hundredths.' So five percent of something is the same as five hundredths of something. That really makes *sense*."

Think About This

The words *percent* and *cent* come from the Latin word *centum*, meaning "hundred." Think of other words that have *cent* as part of the word, meaning "hundred" or "hundredth."

Cents and Fractions

Kazu was counting the change in her purse. She noticed the different types of coins.

"Here's a quarter, 25 cents. Four quarters make a dollar, so each quarter is worth a fourth of a dollar. A fourth is the same as a quarter. I guess that's why it's called a quarter."

Ron looked up from his book. "And a penny is worth one cent. A hundred pennies make a dollar. Each penny is one hundredth of a dollar. That's why it's called a cent, from the Latin word that means 'hundred.'"

Kazu continued. "A dime is worth 10 cents, or one tenth of a dollar. I wonder why we don't have a coin for one third of a dollar. Let's figure out what a third of a dollar would be worth in cents. We can use my calculator."

Kazu wanted to change the unit fraction ⅓ to a decimal fraction. She pressed the keys:

$$1 \div 3 = 0.3333333$$

"No wonder we don't have a coin worth one third of a dollar. You can't really say exactly how many cents it's worth. The number goes on and on."

Kazu had discovered *repeating decimals*. If her calculator had room for a hundred places, her display would show ninety-nine "threes" after the decimal point. We can write the number:

$$0.333 \ldots \textit{(the dots mean that the number never ends), or}$$

$$0.\overline{3} \textit{ (the bar over the three means that the three is repeated forever).}$$

Kazu decided to use her calculator to change the form of the unit fractions (fractions with the numerator *one*) to decimal fractions. She made a list on a sheet of paper

$$½ = 0.5$$
$$⅓ = 0.33333 \ldots$$
$$¼ = 0.25$$
$$⅕ =$$
$$⅙ =$$
$$⅐ =$$
$$⅛ =$$
$$⅑ =$$
$$1/10 =$$
$$1/11 =$$
$$1/12 =$$

Try This

1. Copy Kazu's list and complete it by changing the unit fractions to decimal fractions. You may want to add more unit fractions to the list. Keep your list for later activities.

2. Some decimal fractions are terminating and some are repeating. A *terminating decimal* has an end, like 0.25. A *repeating decimal* goes on forever, like 0.3333. . . . Name the other terminating decimal fractions in the list.

3. Name the repeating decimal fractions in the list.

4. Examine the denominators of the fractions that have terminating decimal forms. What are the prime factors of these denominators?

Going in Circles

Kazu couldn't decide whether the decimal fraction for $\frac{1}{7}$ was terminating or repeating. The calculator display showed:

$$1 \div 7 = 0.1428571$$

It seemed that it might be repeating, but with so many digits! She decided to use pencil and paper to divide one by seven. She kept at it until she had 14 decimal places in the answer: 0.142857142857, and the remainder was one.

Now she could answer the question; it is repeating. The digits that are repeated are 142857.

$$\frac{1}{7} = 0.\overline{142857}$$

Where had she seen that set of digits before? She showed them to Tom. He recognized them right away. "Those are the digits in the number trick!" (page 100).

They decided to use their calculators to find the decimal fractions for $\frac{1}{7}$, $\frac{2}{7}$, $\frac{3}{7}$, $\frac{4}{7}$, $\frac{5}{7}$, and $\frac{6}{7}$.

They both keyed their calculators for $\frac{2}{7}$:

$$2 \div 7 =$$

Surprise! Tom's display showed 0.2857142. Kazu's display showed 0.2857143. Why did one answer end in 2 and the other end in 3? Tom worked it out with paper and pencil. His answer was 0.285714285714, with the remainder 2.

$$\frac{2}{7} = 0.\overline{285714}$$

Kazu's calculator had rounded up the last digit to a 3.

Kazu and Tom guessed that those six digits were going to be repeated for all the fractions, except that each decimal fraction would start with a different digit. The digits would move around in circles.

Try This

Find the decimal fraction for each of the common fractions: $\frac{3}{7}$, $\frac{4}{7}$, $\frac{5}{7}$, $\frac{6}{7}$. Did Tom and Kazu guess correctly? Did the same six digits move around in a circle?

Our Base-10 System of Numbers

Tom, Ron, and Kazu wondered how they would know whether a common fraction would become a repeating decimal fraction or a terminating decimal fraction. Was there some way to analyze the common fractions?

They wrote the denominators of some unit fractions that have terminating decimal form (see page 104). They were 2, 4, 5, 8, 10. They noticed that the *prime factors* of all these denominators were just two numbers: two and five.

What is the connection between the numbers two and five to the base-10 number system? That's easy: 10 equals 2 times 5.

The three friends made an educated guess, called a *hypothesis*:

Their hypothesis was this: If the denominator of a fraction has the prime factors two and/or five, and no other, its decimal fraction is terminating. If not, the decimal fraction is repeating.

They decided to test the hypothesis on other fractions that had two and five as prime factors of the denominator.

$$3/8 = 0.375 \qquad 3/20 = 0.15$$
$$7/25 = 0.28 \qquad 5/16 = 0.3125$$

The hypothesis seemed to be correct so far.

How about repeating decimals? They decided to test $2/6$, $3/6$, $4/6$, $5/6$.

$$2/6 = 0.333 \ldots \qquad 3/6 = 0.5$$
$$4/6 = 0.666 \ldots \qquad 5/6 = 0.8333 \ldots$$

It didn't work, because $3/6 = 0.5$, a terminating decimal.

"Wait a minute," said Ron. "Maybe the common fraction must be reduced to lowest terms. We know that $3/6$ is the same as $1/2$."

They agreed that what Ron said made good *number sense*. They tried other fractions: $2/15$, $3/15$, and $4/15$. Ron seemed to be on the right track.

They changed their hypothesis to: If the denominator of a fraction reduced to lowest terms has the prime factors two and/or five, and no other, its decimal fraction is terminating. If not, the decimal fraction is repeating.

Try This

1. Test other fractions to find out whether their decimal form is terminating or repeating.

2. Is it possible for a decimal fraction to be neither terminating nor repeating?

Numbers Grow, and Grow, and Grow

What's in This Chapter

Numbers grow in many ways. Some grow by adding a one to a number repeatedly, as for Hanukkah candles or the days of Christmas in the Christmas carol "The Twelve Days of Christmas." Some grow by doubling, like those nasty bacteria that make people sick. The number of a person's ancestors also doubles each generation back. Guess how many ancestors you have going back 2,000 years—more than the number of people who have ever lived! You will also read an old English riddle that is very much like a riddle in an ancient Egyptian papyrus. Last, you will learn how your pennies can grow to help UNICEF save thousands of children's lives every day.

Hanukkah Candles

It was the month of December, the month of holidays, the month that ended with school vacation. First Jonathan and Michael prepared for a Hanukkah celebration at Jonathan's house. This eight-day holiday, the Jewish Festival of Lights, celebrates an event that happened in the year 165 B.C.E., over 2,000 years ago. At that time the brave Maccabees recaptured the temple of Jerusalem from the Syrians. It is said that although there was hardly enough oil to keep the lamps burning for just one night, somehow the oil lasted for eight days.

To celebrate this holiday, one candle is lit the first night, two the second night, three the third night, and so on for each night of the holiday. On the last night, eight candles burn in the candle holder, called the *menorah*. In addition, one candle each night is used to light the others.

Jonathan and Mike figured out how many candles they would need. "We must add one plus two plus three plus four plus five plus six plus seven plus eight." Jonathan wrote the numbers on a sheet of paper and started to add.

"Don't forget," said Mike, "that we'll need an extra candle every night to light the others. That's eight more candles."

Try This

How many candles did the boys need? Did you find a shortcut for getting the sum?

The Twelve Days of Christmas

Soon after the end of Hanukkah, the boys sang Christmas carols. After adding the number of candles that they would need for Hanukkah, Mike and Jonathan decided to add the number of gifts described in "The Twelve Days of Christmas," a very old cumulative Christmas carol from England. In a cumulative song, you add a new line each time, and repeat all the previous lines. Here are the words of the song:

On the first day of Christmas my true love sent to me,

A partridge in a pear tree.

On the second day of Christmas my true love sent to me,

Two turtledoves and a partridge in a pear tree.

On the third day of Christmas my true love sent to me

Three French hens, two turtledoves, and a partridge in a pear tree.

On the fourth day of Christmas my true love sent to me,

Four calling birds, three French hens, two turtledoves, and a partridge in a pear tree.

On the fifth day of Christmas my true love sent to me,

Five golden rings,

Four calling birds,

Three French hens,

Two turtledoves,

And a partridge in a pear tree.

Add a new gift each day, and repeat all the previous days' gifts. The song ends on the 12th day of Christmas, when all 12 gifts are listed. The first part, up to the fifth day, is written out in full. For the sixth day, they sing:

On the sixth day of Christmas, my true love sent to me,

Six geese a-laying,

Five golden rings, . . .

then repeat all the previous gifts.

Six geese a-laying,

Seven swans a-swimming,

Eight maids a-milking,

Nine ladies dancing,

Ten lords a-leaping,

Eleven pipers piping,

Twelve drummers drumming . . .

The boys remembered how they figured out the number of candles they needed for Hanukkah, and that they had added eight extra candles for lighting the others. It would be easy to find the total number of gifts for the 12 days.

Try This

How many gifts were given over the 12 days of Christmas?

Think About This

Were you able to find a shortcut for the addition of the numbers 1 to 12? In the next activity, you will learn a clever way to add the numbers.

Young Gauss, the Math Genius

This story is told about Karl Friedrich Gauss, the great German mathematician. Born in 1777, son of a stonecutter, he went to a local school for the children of working people.

It is not certain whether Gauss was 7 or 10 years old when this incident took place. The class was getting out of control, and the teacher gave them busy work to keep them quiet. The assignment was to add all the numbers from 1 to 100. But young Karl came up with the answer in a minute. How did he do it?

Let's first find a short way to add the numbers from 1 to 10, a method that will also work for larger sets of numbers.

Make pairs of numbers and find their sums. Start by adding the first number and the last number: 1 + 10 = 11.

Work from either end to add pairs: 2 + 9, 3 + 8, 4 + 7, 5 + 6. The sum is 11 for each pair. The number of pairs is five, or half of the last number.

The sum of all the numbers from 1 to 10: 5 × 11 = 55. Check it out.

Try This

1. Use Gauss's method to find the sum of the numbers from 1 to 12, and the numbers from 1 to 20. Check your sums by adding the numbers.

2. Now use the method to find the sum of the numbers from 1 to 100.

Think About This

Will this method work for the sum of the numbers from 1 to 15? When you try to pair up all the numbers, which number is left out? Try to figure out a method that will work for an odd number of *addends* (numbers to be added together).

Multiply by Dividing

"What multiplies by dividing?" Mike challenged Jonathan with this question.

"That's impossible," replied Jonathan. "I know that multiplication and division are opposites. To multiply by dividing is *nonsense*. What's the answer?"

Mike laughed. "Bacteria, microbes, germs. You can't see them, but some of them can make you sick or even kill you. They are one-celled little bugs. Each bacterium divides into two cells every hour, or whatever."

"Wow, that's awesome! How many germs will a single cell split into in 10 hours, if they divide every hour? It must be an awful lot."

Jonathan and Mike decided to figure out how many bacteria would result if a single cell divided in two every hour for 10 hours. They made a table to keep track of their calculations.

Hours	Number of Bacteria
0	1
1	2
2	4
3	8
4	16

When the boys had finished their table, they were really impressed. Over 1,000 bacteria from just one cell in 10 hours!

Try This

Complete the table for 10 hours. How many bacteria are there at the end of 10 hours?

More Bugs

Mike and Jonathan wondered how many bacteria there would be at the end of 20 hours. Maybe they could find a shortcut. Doubling, or dividing into two parts, is the same as multiplying by two. How was the number of hours related to the number two?

They soon saw the pattern. For example:

At the end of two hours: 2 × 2 bacteria
At the end of three hours: 2 × 2 × 2 bacteria
At the end of six hours: the product of six 2s
At the end of 10 hours: the product of 10 2s

They remembered that they knew an easy way to write these products. They could use *exponents*, with the number 2 as the *base*. They needed to figure out the *powers* of 2.

$$2 \times 2 = 2^2$$
$$2 \times 2 \times 2 = 2^3$$
$$2 \times 2 \times \ldots \times 2 \ (10 \ factors) = 2^{10}$$
$$2 \times 2 \times \ldots \times 2 \ (20 \ factors) = 2^{20}$$

To find the number of bacteria in 20 hours, they would need to find the product of 20 twos, or 2^{20}.

But it was almost time for Mike to go home. "Let's just get an idea about how big that number is. We'll estimate it." They knew that 2^{10} was a little more than 1,000. They figured:

2^{20} is the same as [2 × 2 × . . . (10 factors)] × [2 × 2 × . . . (10 factors)], or $2^{10} \times 2^{10}$

They thought that a good estimate is 1,000 × 1,000 = 1,000,000. The actual number is a little more than a million bacteria at the end of 20 hours, and that's not even one day!

Try This

Find the exact number of bacteria at the end of 20 hours.

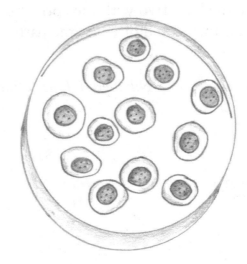

Bugs Multiply Even Faster

When Mike saw a headline in the newspaper about bacteria in hospitals, he read the article and told Jonathan about it.

"I read about bacteria that doubled every half hour, not every hour. The article called a half hour the doubling time."

Jonathan was surprised. "That's even worse than we thought. How many bacteria can one of these bacteria cells produce in 10 hours? Do you think it would be twice as many as the bacteria we talked about yesterday, the kind that doubled every hour?"

The boys decided to find out. Again they made a table. They called the new bacteria Type B and yesterday's bacteria Type A. This time they wrote the base two with the correct exponent, so that they could discover the pattern.

Hours	Number of Type B Bacteria
0	1
½	$2 = 2$
1	$4 = 2^2$
1½	$8 = 2^3$
2	$16 = 2^4$

They could see that in two hours one Type B cell could produce as many bacteria as Type A had in four hours. It took only half the time for Type B to arrive at the same number of bacteria as Type A.

Try This

1. Continue the Type B table for five hours. How many bacteria have been produced at the end of five hours?
2. Estimate the number of Type B bacteria at the end of 10 hours.

Think About This

The number of *E. coli* bacteria can double every 20 minutes. How long will it take for one *E. coli* cell to produce about a thousand bacteria? Estimate the number of bacteria at the end of 10 hours.

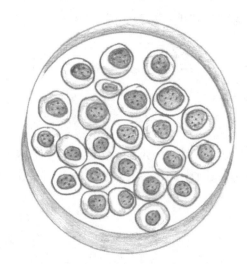

How Many Ancestors?

Jonathan was thinking about all the descendents that came from just one single cell dividing into two cells over and over again. That made him think about his two parents, four grandparents, eight great-grandparents, and his other ancestors, all the way back in time.

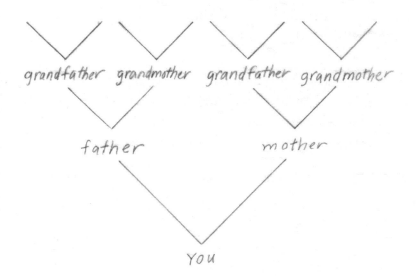

"Let's figure out how many ancestors we have, going back about 200 years," he proposed to Mike.

"What information do we need?" asked Mike, ready to get to work on the project.

"We should have some idea about the number of years in one generation, like how old a person's parents are when that person is born. Just kind of an average number of years."

"When I was born, my mother was 29 and my father was 35," said Mike.

"My parents were both 31 years old when I was born. Let's say that the average number of years in a generation is 33, so there are about three generations in a hundred years. That's an easy number to work with."

"OK, we want to go back 200 years. That's six generations. Let's make a table. We'll need to know how many ancestors are in each generation and the total number of ancestors."

Number of Generations	Number of ancestors This generation	Total
1	2	2
2	$4 = 2^2$	6
3	$8 = 2^3$	14
4	$16 = 2^4$	30
5	$32 = 2^5$	62
6	$64 = 2^6$	126

Mike and Jonathan each had 126 ancestors, going back about two centuries.

Think About This

1. Calculate the number of your ancestors in the 10th generation before you. How can you use that number to calculate the total number of your ancestors going back 10 generations?

2. Jonathan's father became interested in the problem and did some calculations on his computer. He wondered how many ancestors a person had, going back 60 generations, about 2,000 years. The number came out to be more than 2,000,000,000,000,000,000,000.

"But that's *nonsense*!" he said. "There have never been that many people on this planet since the beginning of time!"

How do you explain the contradiction?

The King's Chessboard

Jonathan's sister Sarah had just finished reading *The King's Chessboard*, by David Birch. It's a tale that is popular in China, India, Iran, and other Asian countries. One form of the story tells about a wise old man who showed the king the solution to a problem that no one else had been able to solve. The king was overjoyed and said, "Ask for anything you desire!"

The wise man replied, "Sire, I am old and my needs are few. Just bring a chessboard of 64 squares. Give me one grain of rice for the first square, two grains for the second square, four for the third square, and continue to double the number of grains for each square up to the 64th square."

The king was surprised that the wise man was asking for so little. He could not convince the old man to request palaces or gold.

The treasurer was ordered to have the rice delivered. Soon the king's men had brought all the rice in the kingdom, but that was not enough. It became clear that all the rice in the world would not be enough to fulfill the request. The wise man had made his point, and renounced his request.

Try This

1. How many grains of rice should the man receive for the 11th square?

2. Use the approximate number 1,000 instead of $2^{10} = 1,024$. How much rice would be needed for the 61st square? The 64th square?

Double the Allowance

All these ideas about doubling numbers gave Jonathan an idea. He said to his sister Sarah: "Suppose you could choose how much allowance you could have every month." He gave her these choices:

- Ten dollars at the beginning of the month, or
- One cent the first day of the month, 2¢ the second day, 4¢ the third day, 8¢ the fourth day, and keep doubling until the end of the month.

Sarah thought for a few minutes. At last she decided, "I'll take $10 at the beginning of the month. It's too much work to carry all those pennies."

"Sarah, that's *nonsense*! Do you know how fast numbers grow when they are doubled? Remember that story about the king's chessboard?"

Jonathan made a table to prove his point. Sarah helped with the numbers.

Day	Amount of Money	
	This day	Total
1	$0.01	$0.01
2	0.02	0.03
3	0.04	0.07
4	0.08	0.15
5	0.16	0.31
6	0.32	0.63

On the 30th day Sarah would receive $5,368,709.12, for a total of $10,737,418.23 for the month.

Try This

1. How many days would pass until Sarah received a total of $10?

2. In a 31-day month, how much would Sarah receive on the last day of the month? Use the pattern and numbers already given to find the amount.

Going to St. Ives

Mike came across this old English riddle in a book of nursery rhymes:

As I was going to St. Ives
I met a man with seven wives.
Every wife had seven cats,
Every cat had seven kits,
Every kit caught seven mice.
Kits, cats, mice, and wives,
How many were going to St. Ives?

Mike was puzzled. Should he include the man himself when counting up the number in the group? Without the man, he counted 2,800 individuals; 2,801 if he included the man.

Mike read the verses again and had another question. The man whom the storyteller met might have been going in the direction toward St. Ives, or in the opposite direction. If in the opposite direction, then the storyteller was the only person going to St. Ives.

In the same book of riddles Mike found this interesting information. In an ancient Egyptian papyrus, called the Ahmose papyrus, written about 1650 B.C.E., appeared the following set of figures:

houses	7
cats	49
mice	343
ears of grain	2,401
measures of grain	16,807
Total	19,607

Mike wondered whether the old English nursery rhyme had come down from the ancient Egyptians. We'll probably never know.

Try This

Find the numbers of wives, cats, kits, and mice in the English rhyme. Compare them with the numbers in the Egyptian papyrus. Do they agree?

Pennies Grow to Save Lives

"I know a good project for our class," Jonathan said to Mike. "My mom got a letter from UNICEF. That's the United Nations Children's Fund. It helps children all over the world."

"I know about UNICEF," said Mike. "My mother sends UNICEF cards to her friends. UNICEF raises money that way."

"Well, the letter told about saving lives. Thousands of lives. It was about ORT, Oral Rehydration Therapy. Six thousand babies die every day because of diarrhea. A mixture of salts, sugar, and clean water can save them."

"That sounds simple and cheap," replied Mike.

Jonathan laughed. "Do you know what it costs? Only 12 cents for a treatment. Imagine saving a baby for just 12 cents!"

"We can save a lot of babies. What would it cost to save 6,000 children? Let's figure it out in our heads."

This is how Jonathan and Mike figured the cost of saving 6,000 children:

To save 10 children: 10 times 12¢ = 120¢

To save 100, or 10 × 10 children:
  10 times 120¢ = 1,200¢ = $12.00
To save 1,000, or 10 × 100 children:
  10 times $12 = $120.
To save 6,000, or 6 × 1,000 children:
  6 times $120 = $720.

The boys thought that their class could raise $120, enough to save 1,000 babies. They decided to discuss it with their teacher the next day.

Try This

These are costs of treatment for one child. Use mental arithmetic to figure out the cost for 1,000 children. Watch the decimal points!

Measles vaccine—14¢
Vitamin A to prevent blindness—6¢
Nutrition for one week—$1.45

Numbers grow very fast when many people pitch in. You, your schoolmates, and their families can make a big difference in the world when you all pull together to help children in need. See page 133 for the UNICEF address.

Answers to Selected Questions

Chapter 1
Odds and Evens

p. 6   The Dating Problem: August 28, 888

p. 11   Using *Number Sense*:
"Open Book Puzzles" —numbers 1 and
3 make sense.
"How Many Boys. . ."—number 2
makes sense.

Chapter 2
Prime and Not Prime

p. 19   Number Rectangles:
1. 2, 3, 5, 7, 11
2. 2, 4, 6, 8, 10, 12. Even numbers
3. 12

pp. 22 All About Numbers:
1. 1, 4, 9, 16, 25
2. 2, 3, 5, 7, 11, 13, 17, 19, 23
3. 4, 9, 25
4. 12, 18, 20
5. The number is a square.
6. (a) 3, 6, 9, 12, 15, 18, 21, 24
   (b) 5, 10, 15, 20, 25
7. 15
8. 1, 2, 4, 5, 10, 20, 25, 50, 100;
   5 rectangles

p. 24   What's Odd . . . ?:
Sum of the odd numbers, starting with
one, is a square

Chapter 3
Zero: Is It Something? Is It Nothing?

p. 46   The Missing Year
    1. Three years
    2. Four years

Chapter 4
Money, Measures, and Other Matters

p. 52   The Better Deal:
The eight-ounce carton costs a bit more than 6¢ per ounce. The six-ounce carton costs a bit less than 6¢ per ounce, and is a better deal.

p. 56   Riddle Number Three:
    1. 2 quarters, 1 dime, 8 nickels; 1 quarter, 5 dimes, 5 nickels
    2. 9 dimes, 2 nickels

Chapter 5
Riddles, Puzzles, and Other Mind Bogglers

p. 67   Keisha's Collection:
    1. (a)
    2. 10 cards
    3. 5 rabbits, 15 chickens
    4. There is no biggest number; you can always add to any number or multiply it.

5. $\dfrac{6}{8} \rightarrow \dfrac{6}{8}$

6. $8 \rightarrow 3$; $8 \rightarrow 0$

7. $\text{XII} \rightarrow \text{VII}$

8. $\text{I+I+II} \rightarrow \text{I4I} - \text{II}$
($141 - 11 = 130$)

9. 1, 2, 4, and 8 lb.; add 16 lb.
11. 1,000,000; rub out the one
12. 4:20 PM

p. 71   Guess the Digit:
Notice that the sum of the digits in the answer is always 9.

p. 72   Guess Two Digits
Four names, on pages 99, 198, 297, and 396. Hint: What number is always in the tens place in the answer? What is the sum of the ones digit and the hundreds digit?

p. 73   Calendar Trick
    1. 9 × middle number
    2. 3 × middle number

p. 74   Calendar Magic Square:
Notice that the center row and the center column of the calendar square become the two diagonals of the magic square. The order of the numbers may change.

Chapter 6
Counting

p. 82   Names for Numbers: Base Ten:
17, 50, 13, 18, 44, 14, 17, 65

p. 83   Names for Numbers: Base Twenty:
1. Maya: 200, 80; Yup'ik: 80, 60; Igbo: 200, 60
2. $146 = 7 \times 20 + 6$; $235 = 11 \times 20 + 15$; $399 = 19 \times 20 + 19$

p. 85   Numbers in Stone:
1. 1, 10, 12, 23, 46, 81
3. 612, 250, 1,306, and 3,020

p. 87   Chinese Stick Numerals:

1.   IIII, ΠΠ, =, 40, ☰, ⊥, 80

2. 437; 2,910

p. 88   Chinese Abacus:
12,059; 53,680

p. 90   Inca Quipu: 1. 330

p. 92   Bars and Dots of the Maya:
80, 147, 202, 315, 399

Chapter 7
Calculator

p. 105   Cents and Fractions:
2. $\frac{1}{5} = 0.2$, $\frac{1}{8} = 0.125$, $\frac{1}{10} = 0.1$
3. $\frac{1}{3} = 0.\overline{3}$, $\frac{1}{6} = 0.1\overline{6}$, $\frac{1}{7} = .\overline{142857}$
$\frac{1}{9} = 0.\overline{1}$, $\frac{1}{11} = 0.\overline{09}$, $\frac{1}{12} = 0.083\overline{3}$

p. 107   Our Base-10 System:
2. Yes. For example, pi = 3.14159265 . . . and never repeats. *Pi* is the ratio of the circumference to the diameter of a circle. We use approximate values for pi, such as 3.14 or 22/7.

Chapter 8
Numbers Grow

p. 110   Hanukkah Candles:
44 candles

p. 112   The Twelve Days of Christmas:
364 gifts

p. 113   Young Gauss:
3. The sum of numbers 1 to 100 is 5,050.

p. 114   Multiply by Dividing:
1,024

p. 115   More Bugs:
1,048,576

p. 116   Bugs Multiply Even Faster:
1. 1,024
2. more than a million
Think About This:
$3\frac{1}{3}$ hours; more than 1,000,000,000

p. 117   How Many Ancestors:
1. 2^{10} = 1,024; 2 × 1,024 – 2 = 2,046

p. 119   The King's Chessboard:
1. 2^{10} or 1,024
2. (a) $1,000^6 = 10^{18}$ = one followed by 18 zeros; (b) 8 followed by 18 zeros = 8,000, . . . (18 zeros)

p. 120   Double the Allowance:
1. 10 days
2. $10,737,418.24

p. 122   Pennies Grow:
$140, $60, and $1,450

Bibliography

Books for Kids

Most of the books listed here are appropriate for children in the upper elementary grades. The few exceptions are books for younger children, which are mentioned in the text or are unique in dealing with a certain topic. New and wonderful books are coming out all the time—look for them.

For excellent guides to children's books in mathematics, see Thiessen, Matthias, and Smith (1998) and the two books by Whitin and Wilde in the list of books for adults.

Adler, Irving. *Mathematics*. New York: Doubleday, 1990.

Numbers, their history, and their relations to both geometry and computers.

Anno, Masaichiro, and Mitsumasa Anno. *Anno's Mysterious Multiplying Jar*. New York: Philomel Books, 1983.

Beautiful introduction to factorials.

Anno, Mitsumasa. *Anno's Math Games*. New York: Philomel Books, 1987.

Many challenging applications of numbers, cleverly presented.

Ash, Russell. *Incredible Comparisons*. New York: Dorling Kindersley, 1996.

Numbers and illustrations to explore many facets of our physical world.

Barry, David. *The Rajah's Rice: A Mathematical Folktale from India*. New York: Scientific American Books for Young Readers, 1994.

Rice doubles square by square on the chessboard.

Birch, David. *The King's Chessboard*. New York: Dial Books, 1988.

Rice doubles square by square on the chessboard.

Brett, Jan. *The Twelve Days of Christmas*. New York: Putnam, 1990.

Traditional cumulative Christmas carol, beautifully illustrated.

Burns, Marilyn. *The I Hate Mathematics! Book*. Boston: Little, Brown and Co., 1975.

A lot of challenging activities in many branches of math.

———. *Math for Smarty Pants*. Boston: Little, Brown and Co., 1982.

Good activities to develop number sense.

Demi. *One Grain of Rice: A Mathematical Folktale*. New York: Scholastic, 1997.

Another version of doubling the amount of rice day by day.

Enzensberger, Hans M. *The Number Devil: A Mathematical Adventure*. New York: Henry Holt, 1998.

Although this book is intended as a numerical fairy tale for children, its coverage of sophisticated mathematical topics should be of equal value to adults.

Fisher, Leonard Everett. *Number Art: Thirteen 1 2 3s from Around the World*. New York: Four Winds Press, 1982.

History of 13 number systems.

Hutchins, Pat. *The Doorbell Rang*. New York: Greenwillow Books, 1986.

Division and fraction concepts through sharing cookies, for younger children.

Kallen, Stuart A. *Mathmagical Fun*. Edina, MN: Abdo and Daughters, 1992.

Tricks that can be explained mathematically.

Lumpkin, Beatrice. *Senefer: A Young Genius in Old Egypt*. Lawrenceville, NJ: Africa World Press, 1992.

Ancient Egyptian math in the context of an exciting story based on real life in ancient Egypt.

Massin. *Fun with 9umbers*. San Diego, CA: Creative Editions, 1993.

Numbers and measures in history, from ancient Egypt to the present.

McKibbon, Hugh Williams. *The Token Gift*. New York: Annick Press, 1996.

Another version of doubling the grains of rice on a chessboard.

Morgan, Rowland. *In the Next Three Seconds*. New York: Lodestar Books, 1997.

Data about the state of the world presented through concepts of time.

Peterson, Ivars, and Nancy Henderson. *Math Trek: Adventures in the MathZone*. New York: John Wiley, 2000.

For young people with curiosity about many fields of mathematics, from prime numbers to fractals and chaos.

Schmandt-Besserat, Denise. *The History of Counting*. New York: Morrow Junior Books, 1999.

The author, an archaeologist, is an expert on the numeration of ancient Sumer (now Iraq).

Schwartz, David. *How Much Is a Million?* New York: Lothrop, Lee & Shepherd, 1985.

Interesting situations help children understand the magnitude of large numbers.

———. *If You Made a Million*. New York: Lothrop, Lee & Shepherd, 1989.

All about money, from one cent to a million dollars.

Scieszka, Jon. *Math Curse*. New York: Viking, 1995.

A young student is "cursed" with the discovery that math problems are everywhere, but relieved to find that the problems have solutions.

Stienecker, David L. *Numbers*. New York: Benchmark Books, 1996.

A book in the Discovering Math series. History and characteristics of number systems and numbers.

Zaslavsky, Claudia. *Count on Your Fingers African Style*. New York: Crowell, 1980. Reprinted with full-color art: New York: Black Butterfly, 1999.

Counting and cultural background of several African societies, for younger children.

————. *Math Games and Activities from Around the World*. Chicago: Chicago Review Press, 1998.

More than 70 games, puzzles, and projects from all over the world, some centuries old, encourage kids to hone their math skills while they learn about many cultures. For ages eight and up.

Books for Adults

The list below represents a sampling of books for adults, ranging in content from ways to overcome math anxiety and avoidance, to helping children enjoy math, to a discussion of current topics in the field of mathematics.

Butterworth, Brian. *What Counts: How Every Brain Is Hardwired for Math*. New York: The Free Press, 1999.

This book includes how the brain deals with numerical concepts, how systems of numeration developed through the ages, how children learn arithmetic, and much more. Written in an appealing style, with many fascinating examples.

Davis, Philip J., and Reuben Hersh. *The Mathematical Experience*. Boston: Houghton Mifflin, 1981.

Portrays the rich diversity of the world of mathematics in an enlightening and entertaining style.

Frankenstein, Marilyn. *Relearning Mathematics*. London: Free Association Books, 1989.

For those whose early experience turned them away from math.

Fraser, Don. *Taking the Numb Out of Numbers.* Burlington, Ontario: Brendan Kelly Publishers, 1998.

Just what the title implies.

Huff, Darrell. *How to Lie with Statistics.* New York: Norton, 1954.

Still popular after all these years; how numbers are used and misused.

Kaplan, Robert. *The Nothing That Is: The Natural History of Zero.* New York: Oxford University Press, 1999.

Zero through the ages.

Kenschaft, Patricia Clark. *Math Power: How to Help Your Child Love Math, Even If You Don't.* Reading, MA: Addison-Wesley, 1997.

Just what the title says, and a lot more, including pages of resources. Invaluable for parents (and teachers) of children from preschool to upper elementary grades.

McLeish, John. *Number: The History of Numbers and How They Shape Our Lives.* New York: Fawcett Columbine, 1991.

From ancient Mesopotamia to the computer age.

Paulos, John Allen, *Innumeracy.* New York: Hill and Wang, 1988.

A bestseller, this book is a good sequel to Huff's *How to Lie with Statistics.*

Rucker, Rudy. *Mind Tools: The Five Levels of Mathematical Reality.* Boston: Houghton Mifflin, 1987.

Modern mathematics, presented in a light-hearted style.

Steen, Lynn Arthur, ed. *Why Numbers Count— Quantitative Literacy for Tomorrow's America.* New York: The College Board, 1997.

Distributed by NCTM (see Other Resources, page 133).

Stenmark, Jean K., Virginia Thompson, and Ruth Cossey. *Family Math.* Berkeley, CA: Lawrence Hall of Science, University of California, 1986.

Inspires a nationwide service program for parents; very usable by individuals.

Thiessen, Diane, Margaret Matthias, and Jacquelin Smith. *The Wonderful World of Mathematics: A Critically Annotated List of Children's Books in Mathematics* (second ed.) Reston, VA: National Council of Teachers of Mathematics, 1998.

Reviews more than 550 books.

Tobias, Sheila. *Overcoming Math Anxiety*. New York: Norton, 1993.

Now a classic; addressed mainly to middle-class white women.

Whitin, David J., and Sandra Wilde. *Read Any Good Math Lately? Children's Books for Mathematical Learning, K–6*. Portsmouth, NH: Heinemann, 1992.

—————. *It's the Story That Counts: More Children's Books for Mathematical Learning, K–6*. Portsmouth, NH: Heinemann, 1995.

How to use children's books with the greatest effectiveness.

Zaslavsky, Claudia. *Africa Counts: Number and Pattern in African Cultures*. Chicago: Lawrence Hill Books, 1973, revised 1999.

A fascinating study of mathematical thinking among African peoples living south of the Sahara. Discusses numeration systems, applications of numbers, geometric patterns in art and architecture, games, and much more.

—————. *Fear of Math: How to Get Over It and Get on with Your Life*. Piscataway, NJ: Rutgers University Press, 1994.

Societal factors that lead to fear and avoidance of math, particularly among women and people of color. Includes personal interviews and applications of math in our own lives.

—————. *The Multicultural Math Classroom: Bringing in the World*. Portsmouth, NH: Heinemann, 1996.

Primarily for teachers, but of value to parents who want a multicultural curriculum for their children.

Other Resources

National Council of Teachers of Mathematics (NCTM). 1906 Association Drive, Reston, VA 22091-1593; www.nctm.org. Call (800) 235-7566 to order materials and current catalog of publications and other resources. Publishers of four journals for teachers, including *Teaching Children Mathematics* for the elementary grades. The NCTM Standards documents are very influential; see *Principles and Standards for School Mathematics* (2000).

UNICEF. United Nations Children's Fund. 333 E. 38th Street, New York, NY 10016; www.unicefusa.org. (800) 367-5437 or (800) 252-5437 for the Trick-or-Treat program. Offers educational materials and kits for fundraising and other activities. Issues annual *State of the World's Children* (Oxford University Press).

Index

Alignment with the National Council of Teachers of Mathematics 2000 *Standards*

Content Standards

N = Number and Operations
A = Algebra
G = Geometry
M = Measurement
D = Data Analysis and Probability

Process Standards

P = Problem Solving
R = Reasoning and Proof
C = Communication
CN = Connection
RP = Representation

1. Odds and Evens

	N	A	G	M	D	P	R	C	CN	RP
When Is an Even Number Odd? (p. 2)	•	•				•	•	•		
When Is an Odd Number Even? (p. 4)	•	•				•	•	•		
The Dating Problem (p. 6)	•	•				•	•	•		•
Number Sense About Odds and Evens (p. 8)	•	•				•	•	•		
Puzzles About Odd and Even Numbers (p. 11)	•	•				•	•	•		
Multiplication by Doubling (p. 12)	•	•				•	•	•	•	•

2. Prime and Not Prime

	N	A	G	M	D	P	R	C	CN	RP
Number Rectangles (p. 16)			•	•		•	•	•		•
Prime and Composite Numbers (p. 20)	•	•				•	•	•		•
All About Numbers (p. 22)	•	•				•	•	•		
What's Odd About Adding Odd Numbers? (p. 23)	•	•	•	•		•	•	•		•
Hunt for Primes (p. 25)	•	•		•		•	•			•
Those Even Numbers (p. 28)	•	•				•	•			
Factors of a Number (p. 30)	•	•				•	•			
Casting Out Nines (p. 32)	•					•	•			
Your Fingers as a Calculator (p. 33)	•	•				•	•			•

3. Zero—Is It Something? Is It Nothing?

	N	A	G	M	D	P	R	C	CN	RP
That Funny Number (p. 36)	•					•	•	•		
When Is Zero Something? (p. 39)	•						•	•		
Make Your Own Odometer (p. 41)	•		•				•	•		
The Many Uses of Zero (p. 43)	•					•	•	•		
Is 0 a Number or a Letter? (p. 45)	•								•	
The Missing Year (p. 46)	•									•
Who Wrote the First Zero? (p. 47)	•									
Zero Is a Special Number (p. 49)	•	•						•		
What Is a Googol? (p. 50)	•									

4. Money, Measures, and Other Matters

	N	A	G	M	D	P	R	C	CN	RP
Choose the Better Deal (p. 51)	•					•	•	•	•	
Sharing the Apples (p. 53)	•					•	•	•		
Making Sense of the Cents (p. 54)	•			•		•	•	•		
Count the Change (p. 57)	•					•				
A Head for Numbers (p. 58)	•						•	•		
Tom Fuller, the African Calculator (p. 59)	•									
The Missing Dot (p. 60)	•			•						
Number Sense and Common Sense (p. 62)	•						•	•	•	
Whose Foot? (p. 63)	•			•		•	•	•		
An Expensive Mistake (p. 64)	•					•	•	•		

Math Games & Activities from Around the World

"Connects youngsters with 'friends' around the globe and through time in compelling math play."

—Dr. Lorraine Whitman, Executive Director, Salvadori Center

Math, history, geography, art, and world cultures come together in this delightful book for kids. More than 70 math games, puzzles, and projects from all over the world are included. Kids will hone their math skills as they use geometry to design game boards and logical thinking to work out strategies or analyze the outcomes of games of chance. Activities include building a model pyramid, testing the golden ratio of the Parthenon, and working maze-like African network puzzles.

ages 9 & up, 160 pages, 11 x 8½
line drawing throughout
paper, $14.95, 1-55652-287-8

Available at your local bookstore, or call (800) 888-4741